17. following ［前］ ～に続いて ［形］ 次の
18. at the same time ［成句］ 同時に
19. simultaneously ［副］ 同時に
20. thereafter ［副］ その後は

Chapter 5 SUMMARY（要約）

1. in summary ［成句］ 要約すると、要するに
2. to sum up ［成句］ 要するに、要約すれば
3. summarize ［動］ 要約する
4. in short ［成句］ つまり、要するに
5. in other words ［成句］ 言い換えれば
6. in brief ［成句］ 手短に言えば
7. to put it briefly ［成句］ 手短に言えば
8. to conclude ［成句］（文頭で）結論から言うと
9. in conclusion/in closing ［成句］ 最後に結論として
10. finally/lastly ［副］ 最後に
11. as a final note ［成句］ 最後に
12. taking everything into consideration ［成句］ すべてを考慮すると
13. on the whole ［成句］ 全体的に見ると
14. overall ［副］ 全体的に言えば ［形］ 総合的な
15. in closing ［成句］ 締めくくりに
16. as mentioned above ［成句］ 上述のように
17. as discussed previously ［成句］ 前に述べたように
18. accordingly ［副］ その結果、そのために
19. hence ［副］ このような訳で
20. all things considered ［成句］ あらゆることを考えてみると

Chapter 6 CONTRAST（対比）

1. nevertheless ［副］ それにもかかわらず
2. nonetheless ［副］ それにもかかわらず
3. in spite of ［成句］ ～にもかかわらず
4. despite ［前］ ～にもかかわらず
5. even though ［成句］ ～であるけれども
6. although ［接］ ～ではあるが
7. however ［副］ しかしながら
8. while ［接］ しかし一方
9. on the other hand ［成句］ 一方で
10. alternatively ［副］ その代わりに
12. instead of ［成句］ ～の代わりに
13. by/in contrast to/with ［成句］ と比べると
14. on the contrary ［成句］ それどころか、逆に
15. conversely ［副］ 逆に言うと、反対に

16. unlike ［前］ ～とは異なって
17. rather than ［成句］ よりはむしろ
18. yet ［副］ だがそれでも
19. that said ［成句］（文頭で）そうは言っても
20. although this may be true ［成句］ これは本当かもしれないが

Chapter 7 EMPHASIS（強調）

1. especially ［副］ 中でも特に、とりわけ
2. particularly ［副］ 中でも特に、とりわけ
3. indeed ［副］ 確かに、それどころか
4. truly ［副］ 本当に
5. really ［副］ 本当に
6. clearly ［副］ 明らかに
7. undoubtedly ［副］ 明らかに、疑いなく
8. absolutely ［副］ まったく
9. certainly ［副］ 確かに
10. surprisingly ［副］ 驚いたことに、意外にも
11. primarily ［副］ 主として
12. basically ［副］ 基本的に
13. in truth ［成句］ 実は
14. actually ［副］ 実際は
15. in fact ［成句］ 実際のところ
16. above all ［成句］ そして何より
17. significantly ［副］ 大いに、著しく
18. even ［副］ ～今でさえ、今ですら、今でも
19. besides ［副］ その上 ［前］ さらにまた
20. of course ［成句］ もちろん

Chapter 8 CONCESSION（譲歩）

1. although ［接］ ～であるけれども
2. though ［接］ ～であるけれども
3. even if/though ［成句］ 仮定の話として
4. be that as it may ［成句］ 仮にそうだとしても
5. granted (that) ［成句］ 仮に～だとしても
6. despite ［前］ たとえ～だとしても
7. in spite of ［成句］ にもかかわらず
8. regardless of ［成句］ にもかかわらず
9. nevertheless ［副］ それにもかかわらず
10. nonetheless ［副］ それでもなお
11. however ［副］ そうは言うものの
12. for all that ［成句］ とは言うものの
13. still ［副］ それでもやはり
14. it's/that's true, but ［成句］ それはそうだけど
15. at any rate
16. in any case

つなぎ言葉一覧表

よく使われているつなぎ言葉を一覧表にしました。異なる文脈で使われることもあるため、同じつなぎ言葉が他の項目に記載されているものもあります。品詞は、〔副〕副詞〔形〕形容詞〔名〕名詞〔前〕前置詞〔動〕動詞〔接〕接続詞　熟語、イディオムは〔成句〕としてまとめています。

Chapter 1 ADDITION（追加）

1. furthermore〔副〕その上
2. moreover〔副〕その上に
3. additionally〔副〕その上、さらに
4. in addition〔成句〕さらに、その上、加えて
5. besides〔副〕その上〔前〕～以外に
6. also〔副〕同様に
7. likewise〔副〕同様に
8. in the same way〔成句〕同様に
9. similarly〔副〕同じように
10. in addition to〔成句〕～に加えて
11. on top of that〔成句〕それに加えて
12. together with〔成句〕～と一緒に
13. as a consequence〔成句〕結果として
14. as a result〔成句〕結果として
15. specifically〔副〕具体的には
16. conversely〔副〕逆に
17. what's more〔成句〕しかも
18. still〔副〕さらには
19. apart from〔成句〕～を除けば、～以外は
20. consequently〔副〕前述の理由により

Chapter 2 EXAMPLES（例）

1. for example〔成句〕例えば
2. for instance〔成句〕例えば
3. such as〔成句〕例えば～など
4. for one thing〔成句〕一例をあげると
5. as an example of〔成句〕の例として
6. as an illustration〔成句〕実例として
7. demonstrate〔動〕（実例で）はっきり示す
8. illustrate〔動〕を例証する
9. in particular〔成句〕特に、具体的には
10. specifically〔副〕具体的に言うと
11. especially〔副〕特に
12. namely〔副〕すなわち
13. i.e.〔ラテン語 id est の略〕すなわち
14. particularly〔副〕とりわけ
15. including〔前〕～などの
16. in this case〔成句〕この場合は
17. in other words〔成句〕言い換えれば
18. that is (to say)〔成句〕（前をうけて）つまり

19. above all things〔成句〕何よりもまず
20. thus〔副〕上に述べたように

Chapter 3 CONSEQUENCE（結果）

1. therefore〔副〕そうであるから
2. consequently〔副〕その結果として
3. as a result of〔成句〕の結果として
4. hence〔副〕（前述の事実の）結果として
5. as a consequence〔成句〕結果として
6. accordingly〔副〕結果的に
7. in the outcome〔成句〕結果的に
8. thereupon〔副〕その結果
9. eventually〔副〕結局は
10. in the end〔成句〕最後には
11. but all in all〔成句〕だが結果的に
12. for this reason〔成句〕このような訳で
13. as it turned out〔成句〕後からわかったのだが
14. for this purpose〔成句〕このために
15. result in〔複合動詞〕（結果的に）～をもたらす
16. end up with〔複合動詞〕（結果的に）～で終わる
17. prove (to be)〔動〕～であることが判明する
18. well then〔成句〕それだったら
19. but still〔成句〕それでも
20. thus〔副〕（文頭で）だから

Chapter 4 SEQUENCE（順序）

1. first/firstly〔副〕最初に
2. in the first place〔成句〕最初に
3. initially〔副〕最初は
4. at first〔成句〕初めは
5. first of all〔成句〕まず第一に
6. second/secondly〔副〕二番目に
7. third/thirdly〔副〕三番目に
8. next〔形〕次の〔副〕次に
9. last/lastly〔副〕最後に
10. finally〔副〕最後に
11. later on〔成句〕あとで
12. at last〔成句〕最後に
13. for starters / for a start〔成句〕まずは
14. to begin with / to start with〔成句〕まず始めに
15. then〔副〕それから
16. subsequently〔副〕続いて

Tell Your Story!

Using Transition Words in English Writing

つなぎ言葉でみがく英作文

Junji Nakagawa   Joe Alloway   Ayden Harris

photographs by

iStockphoto

音声ファイルのダウンロード／ストリーミング

CD マーク表示がある箇所は、音声を弊社 HP より無料でダウンロード／ストリーミングすることができます。下記 URL の書籍詳細ページに音声ダウンロードアイコンがございますのでそちらから自習用音声としてご活用ください。

https://www.seibido.co.jp/ad696

Tell Your Story!

はじめに

　このテキストは、みなさんが効果的なパラグラフライティングを習得できることを目指して書かれたものです。英語教育の目的には対人コミュニケーションや会話力の育成などもありますが、このテキストは良い英文を書くという異なったアプローチでみなさんの英語力向上に役立つことを願っています。英語力をアップさせ、私生活や仕事で英語を使いたいと思う人なら誰でも、最終的には英作文のスキルの重要性を再認識するはずです。このテキストに掲載されているパラグラフライティングのフォーマットやテクニックを学習し実践すれば、今のあなたのレベルに関係なく、誰もがライティングスキルを向上させることができます。他のすべての分野同様、ライティングにも時間と練習が必要ですが、このテキストをやり遂げた人は、英文ライティングのスキルがアップし自信がついたことを実感できるはずです。

　このテキストでは、ソーシャルメディア、インドアガーデニング、コミックなど、現代的で興味深いトピックを取り上げることで、文章作成能力を養えるよう構成されています。英作文の基礎を学ぶだけでなく、各章で重要な「つなぎ言葉」を紹介し、スムーズな英文ライティングができるように工夫されています。これらのつなぎ言葉は、アイデアをつなげたり、推敲を加えることで、文章の流れをより自然なものにします。また、クラスでの共同作業を通して、さまざまなトピックについて協力して書くこともできます。このテキストの練習問題をこなすことで、自信を持ってメールやパラグラフ、さらにはエッセイを書くことができるようになるでしょう。

　現代社会において、私たちが文章を作成することは多岐にわたる場面で極めて重要な役割を果たしています。しかし、英作文が得意でない場合、その重要性にもかかわらず、苦手意識を抱えることも少なくありません。こうした人たちにも、このテキストを通じて、作文力を向上させ、その弱点を克服していく道を見つけていただきたいと考えています。本書でライティングの技術を磨くことで、自身の思想や感情、考えをより明確に、効果的に表現することができるようになります。また、生成 AI では書けない、個々人の独自の経験や個性が詰まったメッセージを構築することができます。このテキストを修了された後もぜひ、自信をもって楽しみながら英文を書き続け、現代社会の一員としてどんどん活躍できる人になってください。

　本書の出版に際しましては、成美堂の宍戸貢氏と松本風見氏にご尽力いただきました。お二人の支援と指導がなければ、本書は完成しませんでした。執筆者一同、宍戸氏、松本氏の献身的なご助力と貴重なお時間をいただいたことに深く感謝申し上げます。

Junji Nakagawa
Joe Alloway
Ayden Harris

本書の構成と使い方について

本書はつなぎ言葉を効果的に使うことでパラグラフを実際に応用して書く力を磨くことを目的としています。

パラグラフ

一つのテーマに沿って導入文→支持文→結論文で構成された文章のまとまりを言います。また、一つのテーマについて筋道を立てて論じられた主張をまとめたものです。最初の1文は**導入文**（introduction sentence）で、書き手が最も伝えたい意見や考えを主題として述べます。**支持文**（supporting sentences）は、具体的な事柄や事実、例、理由などを示して主題を明確に裏付ける説明をします。それぞれの文章を論理的につなげて、流れのよい構成にしていくのがポイントです。**結論文**（concluding sentence）はこれまでに述べてきたことの最終的なまとめです。導入文と一貫した内容となっています。

つなぎ言葉

文章の論旨を明確に展開する上で、とても重要な役割を果たします。このテキストでは、パラグラフを論理的に組み立てていくのに用いられる典型的な「つなぎ言葉」をタイプ別に各Chapterで取り上げて学習していきます。

パラグラフライティング

一つのパラグラフで一つの主張を論理的に展開していく文章の書き方です。「ライティング」の世界標準の表現スタイルです。

Aim, Target Words & Phrases, WARM-UP

授業が始まる前までに目を通しておきましょう。WARM-UPの語彙の左上の記号A、B、Lは、その語彙が使用されている箇所を示しています。

READING SECTION

Model Reading A と B でパラグラフを読み、「つなぎ言葉」がどのように使われて論旨が展開されているかを学びます。何度も繰り返し読み、英文の構造を理解していきましょう。

Ⅰ．本文の理解度を測るための問題です。文を完成するのに適切な選択肢を選びましょう。

Ⅱ．文法的にふさわしい語形でカッコ内に記述しましょう。

Ⅲ．パラグラフライティングの構成を把握するための問題です。AとBとでは質問の形式が

異なっていますが、問題を解きながらパラグラフの構造を形成する「導入・支持・結論」の順序に徹底的に慣れ、主張の展開の仕方を学びましょう。

Ⅳ．パラグラフにタイトルをつける問題です。パラグラフの中心となる主張をつかんで簡潔に表現する練習を重ねていくと、各章の最後の問題 (Finishing Touches for Chapter) で「テーマ」を設定する際に役立ちます。

LISTENING SECTION

各 Chapter に関連のある話題の会話文です。音声を聞いてリスニング力を養い、カッコ内を完成させたら、発音練習へつなげていきましょう。

WRITING SECTION

Ⅰ．文の中で適切なつなぎ言葉を使えるかどうかを問う問題です。分かりにくいときは、解説やヒントを確認してください。

Ⅱ．和文英訳問題です。与えられたつなぎ言葉をうまく使って英文にしましょう。

Ⅲ．例文にならってオリジナルな文章を書いてみましょう。つなぎ言葉は繰り返し使うことで感覚が養われます。

Ⅳ．各 Chapter の仕上げとなります。自分が表現したいことを自由に楽しんで書けるようになることを主眼としています。AI には書けないあなたの「個性」を活かしたパラグラフを書いてみましょう。

Brush-up Assignment

ここは宿題コーナーです。実際に使われているつなぎ言葉を辞書や新聞、ネットで調べてみましょう。

本書で説明されている手順や活動を実行することで、あなたのライティングスキルは上達していきます。さらに、英語で書くことが楽しくなり、自分の言いたいことが文章を通して相手に伝わるという満足感も得られるに違いありません。このテキストを活用して、あなたの文章力を磨いていき、ますます書くことを楽しんでほしいと願っています。

CONTENTS

Chapter 1

The Midnight Sun Baseball Game

白夜の野球試合

Aim

Transition Words & Phrases for ADDITION

^A as a result（結果として）^A consequently（前述の理由により）^A conversely（逆に）

^B what's more（しかも）^B furthermore（その上）^L moreover（その上に）^L still（さらには）

Core Idea: uncommon sports experiences

※ ^A は Model Reading A、^B は Model Reading B、^L は LISTENING SECTION で扱われています。

◯ WARM-UP ◯

それぞれの語句に合う日本語を選んで、記号を（　）に入れましょう。

1. ^A peculiar（　　　）　　**2.** ^A extreme（　　　）　　　**3.** ^A noticeable（　　　　）

4. ^A nearly（　　　）　　**5.** ^B celebrate（　　　）　　　**6.** ^B longest-running（　　　）

7. ^B local time（　　　）**8.** ^L national pastime（　　　）**9.** ^L Baseball Hall of Fame（　　　　）

10. ^L diehard（　　　）

a. もっとも長く続いている　　b. 国民的娯楽　　c. を祝う　　d. 現地時間　　e. 特有の
f. 極端な　　　　g. 野球の殿堂　　　h. 顕著な　　　i. ほぼ　　　j. 熱狂的な

1

READING SECTION

Model Reading A

Alaska, located at the northwestern tip of North America, is famous for peculiar weather phenomena. As a result of this northern location, Alaska experiences extreme differences in daylight between summer and winter, most noticeable on the solstices. The summer solstice is the year's longest day, and the winter solstice is the shortest.
5 Consequently, on the summer solstice, Fairbanks, Alaska, located in the middle of the state, has nearly 22 hours of daylight. Conversely, the winter solstice has less than four hours of daylight! Because they live in a place with such extreme weather conditions, Alaskans are sure to enjoy nature as much as possible, especially during summer.

> **Notes** ....
> **midnight sun** 白夜 **solstice**（夏至・冬至の）至点（太陽が赤道から北または南にもっとも遠く離れる時。年に２回あり、**the summer solstice**「夏の至点」が「夏至」**the winter solstice**「冬の至点」が「冬至」）

Ⅰ 本文を読んで、下線部に入るもっとも適切なものを a ～ d より選びましょう。

In Fairbanks, the daylight hours are nearly 22 hours long on _____.
   a. the winter solstice   **b.** the solstices   **c.** the summer solstice
   d. any sunny day

Ⅱ 本文の内容と一致するように、（　　）に適切な一語を書き入れましょう。

Alaska is famous for its unique weather (　　　　　　　　).

Ⅲ Model Reading A と同じ内容になるように次の英文を順に並べ替えましょう。

1. For example, Fairbanks has close to 22 hours of daylight on the summer solstice and under only four hours of daylight on the winter solstice.

2. In such harsh weather, Alaskans enjoy nature as much as possible, especially in summer.

3. Alaska is well known for its unique weather events.

4. The summer solstice is the longest day of the year, while the winter solstice is the shortest.

5. Because of its northern location, summer and winter hours of sunlight vary greatly.

   (　　) → (　　) → (　　) → (　　) → (　　)

Model Reading B

 03

The Midnight Sun Baseball Game, held on the summer solstice in Fairbanks, is a unique baseball experience. First, it is one of the longest-running traditions in amateur baseball: the first game was played in 1906 to celebrate the long Alaskan summer days. What's more, it is only ever played with natural light. Furthermore, it starts at 10 PM local time on the summer solstice and ends between two and three AM. Finally, players and fans stand to sing "Alaska's Flag," the Alaska state song, at the end of the inning nearest midnight. All of this makes the Midnight Sun Baseball Game a special experience for baseball fans.

Notes amateur baseball アマチュア野球 "Alaska's Flag"「アラスカの旗」（公式の州歌）

I 本文を読んで、下線部に入るもっとも適切なものを a ~ d より選びましょう。

The Midnight Sun Baseball Game was originally a fun event to _____ in Alaska.

a. celebrate the long summer days   b. keep the longest-running traditions

c. play outside with artificial illumination   d. sing the official state song

II 本文の内容と一致するように、（　　）に適切な一語を書き入れましょう。

The Midnight Baseball Game is played with (　　　　　　　　) light, even though it is held in the middle of the night.

III Model Reading B と同じ内容になるように、次の英文の下線部に適切な語句を書き入れましょう。

Main Idea: The Midnight Sun Baseball Game is a _____ baseball experience.

Supporting Details:

1. _____, it is one of the _____ traditions in amateur baseball.

2. _____, it takes place only in natural light.

3. _____, it starts at _____ and ends between _____.

4. _____, all in attendance stand and sing _____ at close to midnight.

Conclusion: Because of all these elements, the Midnight Sun Baseball Game is a _____ for baseball fans.

Ⅳ Reading A と Reading B にそれぞれ適したタイトルを英語で書きましょう。

Reading A : _____

Reading B : _____

LISTENING SECTION ⟩⟩

Ⅰ 次の会話文を聞いて空欄を埋めましょう。

A: Baseball is America's national pastime, and it's also my (¹ _____) sport.

B: Mine, too! (² _____), there are so many things we baseball fans can experience in our lives.

A: That's true! I would love to watch the World (³ _____) and visit the Baseball Hall of Fame in Cooperstown, New York.

B: Any baseball fan would love those!

A: Right? (⁴ _____), diehard fans go anywhere to have extraordinary baseball experiences.

B: Where would you like to go?

A: I love baseball's history. (⁵ _____), I hope to see the Field of Dreams in Dyersville, Iowa, or maybe the Midnight Sun Baseball Game in Fairbanks, Alaska.

B: Sounds great. Going to those less famous historical baseball places and games would be a (⁶ _____) memory.

Ⅱ 質問を聞いて、正しい答えを a ～ c より選びましょう。

1. a   b   c

2. a   b   c

WRITING SECTION

✔ 「追加」のつなぎ言葉をうまく使うためのヒント

「追加」のつなぎ言葉は、直前に述べた文について、説明を加えたり、足りない点を補うときに使用します。前に述べたことを受けて主に文頭で使いますが、文中や文末で使うこともあります。また、「追加」のつなぎ言葉は、アイデアをつなぎ合わせたり、自分の主張や観点を裏づけるために、新しい情報を追加したい場合にも便利です。

本文で取り上げた以外に、次のような「追加」のつなぎ言葉があります。

additionally（その上、さらに）**also**（同様に）**apart from**（～を除けば、～以外は）**as well**（同じに）**in addition to that**（それに加えて）**likewise**（同様に）**not only A but (also) B**（AだけでなくBも）**on top of that**（それに加えて）**together with**（～と一緒に）

「追加」のつなぎ言葉の具体的な使い方をみてみましょう。

■文頭での使用例

1. Online games have become more and more popular. **Additionally**, meeting people online has become an everyday occurrence.
   （オンラインゲームの人気が高まってきた。**さらに**、オンラインで人と出会うことが日常化してきた）

2. **Apart from** the occasional disagreement, Haruka and I get along very well.
   （たまに意見が合わないこと**を除けば**、ハルカと私はとても仲がいい）

■文中での使用例

3. He's a gifted singer, and **on top of that**, he's an all-around athlete.
   （彼は歌の才能があり、**その上**、スポーツ万能である）

4. My order arrived today **together with** the instruction manual.
   （注文した商品は、今日、取扱説明書**と一緒に**届いた）

■文末での使用例

5. I finished the project on time. Ken finished on time **as well**.
   （私は時間通りにプロジェクトを完了させた。ケン**も同様に**時間通りに終わらせた）

6. The house is beautiful. The garden is well-maintained, **furthermore**.
   （この家はきれいだ。庭は**さらに**よく手入れされている）

つなぎ言葉は、主に副詞的に使います。前置詞から始まる句は、副詞句になります。また、形容詞の語尾に -ly を付けたものは「副詞」になり、しばしば文全体を修飾します。しかし、lovely や friendly など、名詞に -ly がついた語は形容詞になり、副詞にはなりません。

I 次のそれぞれの英文にもっとも適したつなぎ言葉を下の選択肢から選びましょう。文頭に来る語は大文字で書き始めましょう。

1. I have nothing much to do in the morning (　　　　　　　　) having online meetings.

2. I worked (　　　　　　　　) him on that project.

3. I have completed my homework. (　　　　　　　　), I have studied for my quiz tomorrow.

4. Not only is the learning content important, (　　　　　　　　) the quality of the learning is equally important.

> additionally, but, as a result, apart from, in addition to, together with

---

II 与えられた語句を使って、次の日本語を英語にしましょう。

1. 夏休みにハワイ旅行を計画しています。友人のトムも一緒に行こうと考えています。
(trip to Hawaii, also)

_____

2. 日本では製造業が盛んだが、サービス業も同様に非常に活発である。
(manufacturing, service industry, likewise)

_____

3. このアプリを使えば、メニューがより見やすくなる。それに加えて、操作がとても簡単になる。(app, in addition to that, operate)

_____

Ⅲ Let's practice transitions!

例文にならって , 文を作ってみましょう。

例文

1. (a) The summer solstice is the year's longest day, and the winter solstice is the shortest.

   (b) **Consequently**, on the summer solstice, Fairbanks has nearly 22 hours of daylight!

Your original

   (a) _____

   (b) **Consequently**, _____

   _____

2. (a) Fairbanks, Alaska, has nearly 22 hours of daylight on the summer solstice.

   (b) **Conversely**, the winter solstice has less than four hours of daylight!

Your original

   (a) _____

   (b) **Conversely**, _____

   _____

3. (a) The Midnight Sun Baseball Game was first played in 1906 to celebrate the long Alaskan summer days.

   (b) **What's more**, it is only ever played with natural light.

Your original

   (a) _____

   (b) **What's more**, _____

   _____

Ⅳ Finishing Touches for Chapter 1

次のテーマで一つのパラグラフを英文で書きましょう。

テーマ：私が家族や友だちと経験した貴重な体験

条　件：パラグラフライティングの手法を用いて書く。2つ以上の「追加」のつなぎ言葉を用いる。単語数は 100 words 程度とする。

あなたは Midnight Sun Baseball Game のような、ユニークなゲームやイベントを体験したことはありませんか？　あなたがこれまでに家族や友だちと一緒に体験した貴重な出来事を題材にして、1つのパラグラフにまとめてみましょう。出来上がったら、文書または口頭で発表しましょう。

Paragraph Title: ＿＿＿＿＿＿＿＿＿＿＿＿＿＿＿＿＿＿＿＿＿

Introduction Sentence: ＿＿＿＿＿＿＿＿＿＿＿＿＿＿＿＿＿

＿＿＿＿＿＿＿＿＿＿＿＿＿＿＿＿＿＿＿＿＿＿＿＿＿＿＿

Supporting Sentences: ＿＿＿＿＿＿＿＿＿＿＿＿＿＿＿＿＿

＿＿＿＿＿＿＿＿＿＿＿＿＿＿＿＿＿＿＿＿＿＿＿＿＿＿＿

＿＿＿＿＿＿＿＿＿＿＿＿＿＿＿＿＿＿＿＿＿＿＿＿＿＿＿

＿＿＿＿＿＿＿＿＿＿＿＿＿＿＿＿＿＿＿＿＿＿＿＿＿＿＿

Concluding Sentence: ＿＿＿＿＿＿＿＿＿＿＿＿＿＿＿＿＿

＿＿＿＿＿＿＿＿＿＿＿＿＿＿＿＿＿＿＿＿＿＿＿＿＿＿＿

他にもこんな「追加」のつなぎ言葉があります。

as a consequence（結果として）**as well as**（と同様）**besides**（その上）**further**（さらにまた、その上）**in addition**（さらに、その上、加えて）**in the same way**（同様に）**next**（次に）**similarly**（同じように）**specifically**（具体的には）

Brush-up Assignment

「追加」のつなぎ言葉を使った英文を、辞書や新聞、ネットなどで探して書き出してみましょう。

- ＿＿＿＿＿＿＿＿＿＿＿＿＿＿＿＿＿＿＿＿＿＿＿＿＿＿

＿＿＿＿＿＿＿＿＿＿＿＿＿＿＿＿＿＿＿＿＿＿＿＿＿＿＿

- ＿＿＿＿＿＿＿＿＿＿＿＿＿＿＿＿＿＿＿＿＿＿＿＿＿＿

＿＿＿＿＿＿＿＿＿＿＿＿＿＿＿＿＿＿＿＿＿＿＿＿＿＿＿

Chapter 2

Comic Heroes for the Modern Times

現代のコミックヒーロー

Aim

Transition Words & Phrases for EXAMPLES:

A as an illustration（実例として） A thus（上に述べたように） B for example（例えば）
L specifically（具体的に言うと） L in other words（言い換えれば）

Core Idea: comic heroes

WARM-UP

それぞれの語句に合う日本語を選んで、記号を（　）に入れましょう。

1. A entertainment（　　）　　2. A annual（　　）　　3. A release（　　）
4. A transition（　　）　　5. B contain（　　）　　6. B role model（　　）
7. B complex（　　）　　8. B enduring（　　）　　9. L inspire（　　）
10. L revolutionary（　　）

a. 移行する　　　b. 手本となる人物　　　c. を含む　　　d. 娯楽　　　e. 画期的な
f. 年に一度の　　g. 永続的な　　　h. を奮い立たせる　　i. 複雑な　　　j. 公開

READING SECTION

Model Reading A

 06

 Superhero movies are the most popular entertainment genre of the 21st century. As an illustration, five of the top 10 grossing movies of the 2010s were superhero films. X-Men debuted in July 2000, launching the superhero summer blockbuster in the United States. Summer superhero movies became an annual tradition with the release of Spider-
5 Man in May 2002. From that year on, the first Saturday in May has been called "Free Comic Book Day" in the United States to celebrate that year's new superhero movie. Thus, once considered children's entertainment, superheroes have transitioned into the mainstream over the past 20 years.

> **Notes** genre ジャンル **top 10 grossing movies** 興行収入をあげたトップ **10** の映画 **debut** 初登場する **summer blockbuster** 夏の超大作（アメリカでは **2002** 年の『スパイダーマン』を皮切りに、スーパーヒーローの超大作が毎年夏の定番になっている）

I 本文を読んで、下線部に入るもっとも適切なものを a 〜 d より選びましょう。

X-Men, which debuted in July 2000, was the film that ＿＿＿＿ the summer blockbuster season in the U.S.

　　a. symbolized　　**b.** opened　　**c.** concluded　　**d.** finished

II 本文の内容と一致するように、（　）に適切な一語を書き入れましょう。

Once considered only children's entertainment, superheroes have shifted into the mainstream over the past two (　　　　　　　　　).

III Model Reading A の同じ内容になるように、次の英文を順に並べ替えましょう。

1. Furthermore, with the release of Spider-Man in May 2002, summer superhero movies became a regular feature.

2. In this way, superheroes have moved into the mainstream over the past twenty years.

3. Released in July 2000, X-Men became the biggest summer superhero movie in the U.S.

4. Starting that year, the first Saturday in May has been called "Free Comic Book Day" in the U.S.

5. Since the beginning of the 21st century, superhero movies have become a top entertainment genre.

　　　　（　　　）→（　　　）→（　　　）→（　　　）→（　　　）

Model Reading B

 07

Traditionally considered children's literature, comic books often contain moral messages about life. Before the 1960s, superheroes in comics were generally perfect role models, such as Superman. Marvel Comics reinvented superheroes by creating complex heroes with realistic struggles, despite having superpowers. For example, Spider-Man has super strength and spider-sense but he also has no money and can't keep a girlfriend. Characters with imperfections like these are relatable to children and can teach valuable lessons about living a good life. The enduring popularity of characters created in the 1960s suggests that the lessons they taught then are just as relevant today.

> **Notes** ....
> **Marvel Comics** マーベル・コミック（ニューヨークに本社を置く漫画出版社）**spider-sense** スパイダー感覚（スパイダーマンが持つ危険察知能力）**characters with imperfections** 完璧ではないキャラクター **relatable** 親しみやすい

I 本文を読んで、下線部に入るもっとも適切なものを a ～ d より選びましょう。

Marvel superheroes are relatable to young readers because they have common _____ just like everyone else.

    a. struggles   **b.** adventures   **c.** relationships   **d.** jobs

II 本文の内容と一致するように、（　　）に適切な一語を書き入れましょう。

Comic books have conventionally been viewed children's (   ) in the United States.

III Model Reading B と同じ内容になるように、次の英文の下線部に適切な語句を書き入れましょう。

Main Idea: Comic books often contain _____.

Supporting Details:

1. Prior to the 1960s, superheroes in comics were _____ such as _____.

2. Marvel Comics reworked the superhero by creating _____ with superpowers but also with _____.

3. These non-perfect characters are _____ children and teach them valuable lessons about _____.

Conclusion: The fact that characters created in the 1960s are still _____ shows that what they taught us is _____.

Ⅳ Reading A と Reading B にそれぞれ適したタイトルを英語で書きましょう。

Reading A : _____

Reading B : _____

LISTENING SECTION ▶

CD 08、09

Ⅰ 次の会話文を聞いて空欄を埋めましょう。

A: The X-Men are my favorite Marvel Comic series!

B: Oh, really? I haven't read that comic! Why do you love them (¹)?

A: It's the first comic that showed diversity as a strong point, which is great!

B: Wow! So, the comic can inspire anyone, because of the (²) team of heroes?

A: Exactly! Diversity means that all readers can relate to the story. For (³), a Russian Communist, an African woman, and a Jewish superhero all joined the team over time!

B: It sounds like the X-Men was very (⁴)!

A: I agree! Diversity is a popular (⁵) now, but it was revolutionary in the 1960s. In other (⁶), this comic was decades ahead of its time!

Ⅱ 質問を聞いて、正しい答えを a 〜 c より選びましょう。

1. a   b   c

2. a   b   c

WRITING SECTION

✔ 「例」をあげるつなぎ言葉をうまく使うためのヒント

「例」をあげるつなぎ言葉は、何かをわかりやすく説明するために、例を示したり、具体的な例を あげたりするときに使います。具体例は文脈を明確にするために使うものなので、複雑な言い回し や難しい例は使用しないようにしましょう。

本文で取り上げた以外に、次のような「例」をあげるつなぎ言葉があります。

demonstrate（〔実例で〕はっきり示す）**for one thing**（一例をあげると）**illustrate**（を例 証する）**in particular**（特に、具体的には）**in this case**（この場合は）**namely**（すなわち）

「例」を示すつなぎ言葉の具体的な使い方をみてみましょう。

1. This chapter **illustrates** the basic steps for upgrading a computer with specific examples.

   （この章では、コンピュータのアップグレードの基本的な手順を、**具体的な例をあげて説明します**）

2. Could you **demonstrate** how to use this new app on your phone?

   （この新しいアプリの使い方をスマホで**実演して**いただけませんか？）

3. I'm now going to talk about a major threat facing our society, **namely** a new type of virus.

   （私はこれから、私たちの社会が直面している大きな脅威、**すなわち**新種のウイルスについてお 話しします）

4. It's best to apologize and move on. **In this case**, you definitely won't get into an argument.

   （謝って次に進むのが一番だよ。**この場合**、間違いなく口論になることはないね）

5. I want to improve my public speaking skills. **For one thing**, to be more confident at work.

   （人前で話すスキルを向上させたい。**ひとつには**、仕事でもっと自信を持てるように）

6. He works quickly and efficiently. **In particular**, I'm impressed with his decision-making skills.

   （彼は仕事をテキパキとこなす。**特に**、彼の決断力には感心する）

7. I often listen to upbeat music, rap and hip-hop **in particular**.

   （私はノリのいい音楽、中でもラップやヒップホップ**など**をよく聴く）

For Your Information and Guidance

つなぎ言葉がワンパターン (a single pattern of expression) にならないように、色々な表現のつなぎ言葉を使うことはとても重要なことです。前ページにあげた例文 (7 .) は、こんなふうにも書けます。

1. Examples of upbeat music I listen to most frequently include rap and hip-hop.
2. Rap and hip-hop are examples of upbeat music I listen to most often.
3. I often listen to upbeat music, for instance, rap and hip-hop.
4. I often listen to upbeat music such as rap and hip-hop.

Ⅰ 次のそれぞれの英文にもっとも適切なつなぎ言葉を下の選択肢から選びましょう。文頭に来る語は大文字で書き始めましょう。

1. You need to ( ) by using examples in your presentation to show your approach will yield results.

2. I prefer baseball to soccer. It's not so tiring ( ).

3. This chapter covers several topics, but ( ), focuses on giving examples.

4. The car is stuck in traffic today. ( ), taking the train is faster.

> in particular,   include,   in this case,   examples of,   demonstrate,
> for one thing

Ⅱ 与えられた語句を使って、次の日本語を英語にしましょう。

1. 例えば、宮本武蔵は、歴史小説の代表的な例として広く知られている。
(for instance, historical fiction, prime example)

_____

2. 彼は具体的な事例をあげて、研究内容を聴衆に説明した。
(illustrate, through use of, specific examples)

_____

3. 現代の企業経営は、AI などの新しい技術に対応できないことで倒産するリスクを抱えている。(company management, bankruptcy, such as)

_____

III Let's practice transitions!

例文にならって、文を作ってみましょう。

例文

1. (a) Superhero movies are the most popular entertainment genre of the 21st century.

    (b) **As an illustration**, five of the top 10 grossing movies of the 2010s were superhero films.

Your original

(a) _____

(b) **As an illustration**, _____

_____

2. (a) The first Saturday in May has been called "Free Comic Book Day" to celebrate that year's new superhero movie.

    (b) **Thus**, superheroes have transitioned into the mainstream over the past 20 years.

Your original

(a) _____

(b) **Thus**, _____

_____

3. (a) Marvel Comics created heroes with superpowers but with realistic struggles.

    (b) **For example**, Spider-Man has superpowers, but has no money and can't make a girlfriend.

Your original

(a) _____

(b) **For example**, _____

_____

Ⅳ Finishing Touches for Chapter 2

次のテーマで一つのパラグラフを英文で書きましょう。

> **テーマ**：私の好きなマンガ・アニメのキャラクター
>
> **条　件**：パラグラフライティングの手法を用いて書く。2つ以上の「例」をあげるつなぎ言葉を用いる。単語数は 100 words 程度とする。

教科書では、1960 年代に 21 世紀の理想を描いた X-MEN を賞賛していますが、今日では、こうした古いコミックのファンは少なく、一般的にはもっと現代的な作品に人気があるようです。そこで、その中から特に好きなマンガかアニメを 1 つ選び、その主人公の魅力を 1 つのパラグラフにまとめて紹介しましょう。出来上がったら、文書または口頭で発表しましょう。

Paragraph Title: _____

Introduction Sentence: _____

_____

Supporting Sentences: _____

_____

_____

Concluding Sentence: _____

_____

他にもこんな「例」をあげるつなぎ言葉があります。

above all things（何よりもまず）**as an example of**（の例として）**as illustrated by**（で例示されているように）**especially**（特に）**in the case of**（の場合は）**in this situation**（このような場合）**in this way**（このようにして）**including**（〜などの）**i.e.**（［ラテン語 id est の略］すなわち）**particularly**（とりわけ）**that is to say / that is**（［前をうけて］つまり）

Brush-up Assignment
「例」をあげるつなぎ言葉を使った英文を、辞書や新聞、ネットなどで探して書き出してみましょう。

- _____
- _____

16

Permafrost

永久凍土が溶けてゆく

Aim

Transition Words & Phrases for CONSEQUENCE

[A] as a result of（〜の結果として）[B] as a consequence（結果として）[B] therefore（そうであるから）[L] consequently（その結果として）[L] well then（それだったら）

Core Idea: climate change

WARM-UP

それぞれの語句に合う日本語を選んで、記号を（　）に入れましょう。

1. [A] invisible（　　）　　2. [A] effect（　　）　　3. [A] climate change（　　）
4. [A] be at risk of（　　）5. [A] the Arctic（　　）　6. [B] vast（　　）7. [B] emerge（　　）
8. [B] contribute（　　）　9. [L] atmosphere（　　）　10. [L] increase（　　）

---

a. 広大な　　　b. 影響　　　c. 気候変動　　　d. 増える　　　e. 大気　　　f. 北極圏
g. の危険性がある　　　　h. 出現する　　　i. に貢献する　　　　j. 目に見えない

Model Reading A

 10

One of the invisible effects of climate change is the melting of permafrost. When people think about climate change, they probably consider rising temperatures and storms, but won't imagine climate change melting permafrost in the Arctic. Some areas with permafrost have been frozen for hundreds or thousands of years, but there is less
5 permafrost now than in the past. As a result of rising temperatures, Earth's permafrost is at risk of melting rapidly, which will cause many problems for the entire world. The best way to prevent permafrost from melting is to keep it frozen, but that may no longer be possible in a warming world.

Notes ········· **permafrost** 永久凍土層

Ⅰ 本文を読んで、下線部に入るもっとも適切なものを a 〜 d より選びましょう。

Melting permafrost is mainly a _____ of climate change.
    a. reason   **b.** result   **c.** freeze   **d.** breaking

Ⅱ 本文の内容と一致するように、（　　）に適切な一語を書き入れましょう。

Rapid thawing of the Earth's permafrost along with rising (   ) could cause a variety of problems throughout the world.

Ⅲ Model Reading A の内容と同じになるように、次の英文を順に並べ替えましょう。

1. In fact, there are fewer areas with permafrost than there used to be.

2. One of the effects of climate change is the melting of permafrost.

3. The best way to keep permafrost from melting is to keep it frozen, but it probably won't work.

4. Yet, people don't often imagine that permafrost in the Arctic is melting due to climate change.

5. If temperatures continue to rise, the Earth's permafrost could thaw rapidly.

        (　　) → (　　) → (　　) → (　　) → (　　)

Model Reading B

 11

   Vast areas of permafrost exist in the Arctic that we must preserve. In recent years, permafrost has begun to melt under the influence of climate change. As a consequence, large sinkholes have formed and other dangerous conditions have emerged. Additionally, permafrost releases massive amounts of greenhouse gases as it thaws and decomposes.
5 If global warming proceeds at this rate, all permafrost could thaw completely, affecting the entire ecosystem and the environment. Therefore, we must recognize the risk of permafrost loss and take serious action against global warming. In doing so, we can contribute to the conservation of not only the Arctic but the entire planet.

> **Notes** ┊ **sinkhole** くぼみ、陥没穴 **massive amounts of** 大量の **decompose** 分解する **at this rate** この調子でい
> くと **ecosystem** 生態系 **conservation** 保全

Ⅰ 本文を読んで、下線部に入るもっとも適切なものを a ～ d より選びましょう。

As permafrost disappears, it can leave large ＿＿＿＿＿＿＿ in its place.

    a. streams   **b.** sinkholes   **c.** open spaces   **d.** blocks of ice

Ⅱ 本文の内容と一致するように、（　）に適切な一語を書き入れましょう。

More global warming could affect the (＿＿＿＿＿＿＿＿＿) and the environment of the entire planet.

Ⅲ Model Reading B と同じ内容になるように、次の英文の下線部に適切な語句を書き入れましょう。

Main Idea: The Arctic has enormous areas of ＿＿＿＿＿＿＿＿ which must be ＿＿＿＿＿＿＿＿.

Supporting Details:

1. In recent years, climate change has begun to melt ＿＿＿＿＿＿＿＿, creating dangerous situations.

2. ＿＿＿＿＿＿＿＿, permafrost releases large amounts of ＿＿＿＿＿＿＿＿＿ as it ＿＿＿＿＿＿＿＿ and ＿＿＿＿＿＿＿＿.

3. If global warming continues thus, all permafrost could thaw ＿＿＿＿＿＿＿＿.

4. ＿＿＿＿＿＿＿＿, we must recognize the risk of ＿＿＿＿＿＿＿＿ and take ＿＿＿＿＿＿＿＿ seriously.

Conclusion: This way, we can contribute to preserving ＿＿＿＿＿＿ as well as ＿＿＿＿＿ ＿＿＿＿＿＿＿＿.

19

Ⅳ Reading A と Reading B にそれぞれ適したタイトルを英語で書きましょう。

Reading A : _____

Reading B : _____

LISTENING SECTION ⟩

CD 12、13

Ⅰ 次の会話文を聞いて空欄を埋めましょう。

A. What are the risks of melting permafrost?

B. The top risk would be the release of greenhouse gases such as (¹   )
dioxide and methane from permafrost.

A. What happens if they are (²   )?

B. They will spread into the atmosphere.

A. Consequently, (³   ) will increase, right?

B. That's right. (⁴   ), as the permafrost melts, global warming will
accelerate.

A. Well then, we need to (⁵   ) permafrost as much as we can?

B. Exactly. In the Arctic, they're developing various methods to protect the permafrost
and keep it (⁶   ) as long as possible.

Ⅱ 質問を聞いて、正しい答えを a ～ c から選びましょう。

1. a   b   c

2. a   b   c

WRITING SECTION

✔ 「結果」を述べるつなぎ言葉をうまく使うためのヒント

ある事実から導かれた結末や結論を述べるときに用いるのが「結果」を述べるつなぎ言葉です。このつなぎ言葉を使うと、原因と結果が論理的にはっきりとしてきて、文章の流れが明確になってきます。

本文で取り上げた以外に、次のような「結果」を述べるつなぎ言葉があります。

as it turned out（後から分かったのだが）**but still**（それでも）**end up with**（〔結果的に〕〜で終わる）**eventually**（結局は）**for this reason**（このような訳で）**in the end**（最後には）**in/on the outcome**（結果に）**prove to be**（〜であることが判明する）**result in**（〔結果的に〕〜をもたらす）**so**（だから）**turn out**（結局〔結果的に〕〜になる）

「結果」を述べるつなぎ言葉の具体的な使い方をみてみましょう。

1. Fatigue can **result in** lower work efficiency.
   （疲労は作業効率の低下**をもたらす**）

2. The concert **turned out** to be more enjoyable than I had expected.
   （コンサートは、予想以上に楽しいもの**になった**）

3. He is not satisfied with my idea, **so** I must prepare another proposal.
   （彼は私のアイデアに満足していない。**したがって**、私は別の提案を準備しなければならない）

4. The weather has a tremendous impact **on the outcome** of outdoor games.
   （天候は、屋外での試合の**結果に**多大な影響を及ぼす）

5. I always wear a helmet when riding my bike. **For this reason**, I've never been seriously injured in an accident.
   （私は自転車に乗るとき、必ずヘルメットを装着している。**そのため**、事故で大きなケガをしたことはない）

6. I waited another hour or so, **but still**, she did not show up.
   （さらに1時間ほど待った**が、やはり**彼女は来なかった）

Ⅰ 次のそれぞれの英文にもっとも適したつなぎ言葉を下の選択肢から選びましょう。

1. Our life was going well, (   ), we had a breakdown.

2. This new member will (   ) be a valuable addition to the team.

3. If you decide too quickly, you will be disappointed (   ).

4. As long as you endure this tough training, you will (   ) with excellent results.

> or else,　end up,　prove to,　in the outcome,　so then,　but in the end

Ⅱ 与えられた語句を使って、次の日本語を英語にしましょう。

1. このプロジェクトには幾つかの問題もあったが、結果的には成功した。
   (although, proved to be)

   _____

2. 彼の発言は、結局のところ、日本がグローバルスタンダードから遅れていることを明らかにしている。(eventually, reveal)

   _____

3. 彼女は面接に緊張していたが、後で分かったのだがその場で採用が決まった。
   (nervous about, as it turned out, on the spot)

   _____

Ⅲ Let's practice transitions!

例文にならって、文を作ってみましょう。

例文

1. **As a result of** rising temperatures, Earth's permafrost is at risk of melting rapidly.

Your original

As a result of _____

_____

2. (a) Permafrost has begun to melt under the influence of climate change.

(b) **As a consequence**, dangerous conditions have emerged.

Your original

(a) _____

(b) **As a consequence**, _____

_____

3. (a) If global warming proceeds at this rate, all permafrost could thaw completely.

(b) **Therefore**, we must take serious action against global warming.

Your original

(a) _____

(b) **Therefore**, _____

_____

IV Finishing Touches for Chapter 3

次のテーマで一つのパラグラフを英文で書きましょう。

> **テーマ**：気候変動のリスク
>
> **条　件**：パラグラフライティングの手法を用いて書く。2つ以上の「結果」を述べる
> つなぎ言葉を用いる。単語数は 100 words 程度とする。

永久凍土の融解は、気候変動がもたらす地球規模の変化のひとつに過ぎません。加速する気温や海水面の上昇は、遠く離れた北極圏だけの問題ではなく、日本にも夏の猛暑や熱波、頻発する大規模な自然災害、生態系の破壊といった形で影響を与えています。これらの気候変動によるリスクを減らすために、あなたができることを、事例をあげて1つのパラグラフにまとめてみましょう。出来上がったら、文書または口頭で発表しましょう。

Paragraph Title: _____

Introduction Sentence: _____

_____

Supporting Sentences: _____

_____

_____

Concluding Sentence: _____

_____

他にもこんな「結果」を述べるつなぎ言葉があります。

accordingly（結果的に）**at the end**（最後には）**but all in all**（だが結果的に）**for this purpose**（このために）**thereupon**（その結果）**hence**（[前述の事実の] 結果として）**ultimately**（結局のところ）

Brush-up Assignment
「結果」を述べるつなぎ言葉を使った英文を、辞書や新聞、ネットなどで探して書き出してみましょう。

- _____

_____

- _____

_____

Chapter 4

Indoor Gardening with Hydroponics

インドアガーデニングしませんか

Aim

Transition Words & Phrases for SEQUENCE

^A simultaneously（同時に）^A initially（最初は）^B first of all（まず第一に）^B secondly（二番目に）

^B thirdly（三番目に）

Core Idea: food independence

○ WARM-UP ○

それぞれの語句に合う日本語を選んで、記号を（　）に入れましょう。

1. ^A transport（　　）　　2. ^A income（　　）　　3. ^A on the other hand（　　）

4. ^A cost-effective（　　）5. ^A locally-grown（　　）6. ^B complicated（　　）

7. ^B significant（　　）　　8. ^B component（　　）　　9. ^B straightforward（　　）

10. ^L maintain（　　）

a. 複雑な	b. その一方で	c. を輸送する	d. 重要な	e. 地元産の
f. を維持する	g. 所得	h. 簡単な	i. 費用効率の高い	j. 部品

Model Reading A

 14

    More and more people are trying indoor gardening, so let's look at some of the contributing factors. One concern is the growing carbon pollution caused by the current food supply system, which transports food worldwide daily by planes, trains, trucks, and cargo ships. Simultaneously, many people face rising food costs while their incomes
5 remain unchanged. Indoor gardening, on the other hand, is space-saving, cost-effective, and provides people with locally-grown organic food. Initially designed to grow small plants such as sage and rosemary, the system can now produce as many as 60 different types of plants. These backgrounds have encouraged an increasing number of people to try indoor gardening.

> **Notes** ··
> **contributing factor** 要因　　**food supply system** 食糧供給システム **space-saving** 場所をとらない
> **organic food** 自然食品　**sage** セージ（代表的なハーブのひとつ）**rosemary** ローズマリー（ハーブの一種）

I 本文を読んで、下線部に入るもっとも適切なものを a ～ d より選びましょう。

Whereas indoor gardening was _____ intended for growing tiny plants in the beginning, it can now produce up to 60 different types of plants.
    a. surprisingly   **b.** seriously   **c.** deliberately   **d.** primarily

II 本文の内容と一致するように、（　　）に適切な一語を書き入れましょう。

In the current food supply system, food is transported around the (　　　　) every day by airplanes, trains, trucks, and cargo ships.

III Model Reading A と同じ内容になるように、次の英文を順に並べ替えましょう。

1. Against these backgrounds, people are increasingly adopting indoor gardening.

2. Some are worried about the growing carbon pollution caused by the current food supply system.

3. Consider why more and more people are starting indoor gardens.

4. Indoor gardening, in contrast, takes up less space, is more cost-effective, and allows people to eat locally-grown organic foods.

5. At the same time, many are faced with the problem of rising food costs while their incomes remain the same.

        (　　　) → (　　　) → (　　　) → (　　　) → (　　　)

Model Reading B

 15

Indoor gardening systems may seem complicated, but they are effortless to build, and all you have to do is install three significant components. Now let's take a look at these parts. First of all, every system has a large base with a water pump that holds several liters of water. Secondly, some tubes or pipes may be attached under small plant holders, depending on the design, and moves water to the roots. Thirdly, a grow light device must be fixed or installed near the system. Since all indoor gardening systems are straightforward and the same, anyone can easily install them.

Notes ········· **effortless** 努力を要しない **grow light device** 栽培用照明装置

Ⅰ 本文を読んで、下線部に入るもっとも適切なものを a ～ d より選びましょう。

Indoor gardening systems may seem complicated, but they are actually _____ to put together when you try.

    a. basic   **b.** outdated   **c.** exhausting   **d.** easy

Ⅱ 本文の内容と一致するように、（　　）に適切な一語を書き入れましょう。

To set up an indoor gardening system, you'll need the following pieces of equipment: a grow light, tubes or pipes, and a large base with a (　　) pump.

Ⅲ Model Reading B と同じ内容になるように、次の英文の下線部に適切な語句を書き入れましょう。

Main Idea: Indoor gardening systems may seem _____, but they are _____, and only require _____.

Supporting Details:

1. First, set _____ with a water pump that holds _____.

2. _____, run _____ under _____.

3. _____, connect or place a grow light _____.

Conclusion: Since all indoor gardening systems are _____, anyone can easily _____.

IV Reading A と Reading B にそれぞれ適したタイトルを英語で書きましょう。

Reading A : _____

Reading B : _____

LISTENING SECTION

CD 16、17

I 次の会話文を聞いて空欄を埋めましょう。

A: I heard you started gardening recently; do you like it?

B: Yes, I do. It is (¹) easy, and I have fresh-picked, organic food right in my home.

A: But what about space? Gardens take up a lot of room. How does it fit inside?

B: You'd be surprised! (²), I was also worried, but my system grows thirty plants and takes up very little space.

A: I've heard gardens are time-consuming and (³) a lot of work!

B: Traditional gardens do, yes. Hydroponic gardens are much (⁴).

A: How do they differ?

B: (⁵) from space, they take very little work each week to maintain. Also, the power supply for the lights and water pump is very low, so it is not (⁶).

Notes ┈┈
take up a lot of room 場所をとる **hydroponic garden** 水耕栽培

II 質問を聞いて、正しい答えを a 〜 c から選びましょう。

1. a　　b　　c

2. a　　b　　c

WRITING SECTION

✔ 「順序」を表すつなぎ言葉をうまく使うためのヒント

順序を表す単語やフレーズは、出来事やアイデアの順序を示すときに使用します。first, second…などをパラグラフのなかに挟んでいくと、順番や時間の流れ、重要性の関係が分かりやすくなります。firstly を使ったら次は（second ではなく）secondly というふうに、<u>一貫性をもって</u>使いましょう。

本文で取り上げた以外に、次のような「順序」を表すつなぎ言葉があります。

afterward(s)（その後）**at the same time**（同時に）**but then**（だがその後で）**for now**（今のところ）**for the time being**（当分の間）**next**（次に）**subsequently**（続いて）

first と **firstly**、**last** と **lastly** の具体的な使い方をみてみましょう。

■ **first** vs **firstly**

文中には、first と firstly が使われていますが、使用法の違いをみてみましょう。

first は形容詞と副詞で使われます。

1. He became the **first** president of the company.（形容詞）

   （彼は**初代**社長に就任した）

2. **First**, I will explain the purpose of this meeting.（副詞）

   （**まず**、このミーティングの趣旨を説明します）

一方、**firstly**（第一に、まずはじめに）は副詞でしか使えません。

first を副詞として使う場合は、first → second → third → fourthly → ・・・last と順番にあげていき、**firstly** は firstly (first of all) → secondly → thirdly → fourthly → ・・・lastly/last of all のように、関連する事柄を複数述べていくときに使います。

first と firstly は、状況によっては置き換え可能ですが、すべての場合に当てはまるわけではありません。

3. **First(ly)**, I would like to thank my mother.（first, firstly どちらも使えます）

   （**最初に**、母に感謝をささげたい）

4. I **first** ~~firstly~~ noticed her today.（first「初めて」、firstly は使えません）

   （私は今日、**初めて彼女の存在に気づいた**）

■ **last** vs **lastly**

last は形容詞と副詞で、lastly は副詞です。副詞として使われる場合の last は lastly に置き換えて使うことはできません。

5. It's a long time since we met **last** ~~lastly~~.（副詞）

   （**最後に**会ってからずいぶん経ちましたね）

6. **Lastly**, I want to thank you all for coming.（副詞）

   （**最後になりましたが**、ご来場いただいた皆様、ありがとうございました）

「第一に」「最初に」を表すその他の表現をみてみましょう。

in the (first, second, third, etc.) place （最初に、次に・・・）

　1. そもそも、ほかの何よりも先に

　2. いくつかの項目を列挙して in the first place, second place などと一緒によく使います。

to begin with （まず始めに）**to start with** も同じ

　1. 複数の理由や根拠の1番目を述べるときに使います。

　2. 何かを始めるときに使います。

for starters （まずは）やるべきことやリストの最初にあることを言うときに使います。（**for a start** も同じ）

at first （初めは）あとではそうでなかったという意味を含めて使います。but, then, later などが続くのがふつうです。

Ⅰ 次のそれぞれの英文にもっとも適切なつなぎ言葉を下の選択肢から選びましょう。文頭に来る語は大文字で書き始めましょう。

　1. (　　　　　　　　　　　), I will define the terms I use in this presentation.

　2. Today I will go to the bank first and grocery shopping (　　　　　　　　).

　3. In the first place, she is efficient in her work, and (　　　　　　　), she is attentive to her surroundings.

　4. At first, I wanted Japanese cuisine, (　　　　　　　　) I decided to go Italian.

> but then,　for the time being,　in the second place,　to begin with,
>
> for now,　second

Ⅱ 与えられた語句を使って、次の日本語を英語にしましょう。

　1. そもそも、あなたはそんなことをネットに投稿するべきではなかったのだ。
　　(post, in the first place)

　　_____

　2. まず手始めに、私たちのパソコンを最新のものに買い替えてください。
　　(for starters, replace)

　　_____

　3. 考えるべきポイントは、第一にコスト、第二に時間、第三にスタッフ、の3点である。
　　(firstly, secondly, thirdly)

　　_____

Ⅲ Let's practice transitions!

例文にならって、文を作ってみましょう。

> 例文

1. (a) Airplanes, trains, trucks, and cargo ships transport fresh and canned food worldwide every day.

   (b) **Simultaneously**, many people face rising food costs while their wages remain unchanged.

> **Your original**

    (a) _____

    (b) **Simultaneously**, _____

2. **Initially**, indoor gardening systems were designed to grow small plants such as sage and rosemary, but today they can grow as many as 60 different types of plants.

> **Your original**

    Initially, _____

_____

3. **First of all**, every system has a large base with a water pump that holds several liters of water.

> **Your original**

    First of all, _____

次のテーマで一つのパラグラフを英文で書きましょう。

> **テーマ**：インドアガーデニング（室内園芸）について私が思うこと
>
> **条　件**：パラグラフライティングの手法を用いて書く。2つ以上の「順序」を表すつなぎ言葉を用いる。単語数は 100 words 程度とする。

ここでは環境汚染と物価高の観点から、インドアガーデニングを提唱しています。日本では、異常気象や環境問題のために「食の安全」と「安定供給」が不安視されています。こうした問題解決の一方法として、水耕栽培の植物工場、いわゆる「ベジファクトリー」が出現してきました。あなたは日本の一般家庭で家庭栽培をもっと普及させようという考え方についてどう思いますか？　インドアガーデニングについてあなたの考えを1つのパラグラフにまとめてみましょう。出来上がったら、文書または口頭で発表しましょう。

Paragraph Title: _____

Introduction Sentence: _____

_____

Supporting Sentences: _____

_____

_____

Concluding Sentence: _____

_____

他にもこんな「順序」を表すつなぎ言葉があります。

at last / at the end / in the end（最後に）**finally**（最後に）**following**（〜に続いて）**in conclusion / in closing**（最後に）**in the (first, second, third, etc.) place**（最初に、次に、3番目に…）**last of all**（最後に）**later on**（あとで）**thereafter**（その後は）

Brush-up Assignment
「順序」を表すつなぎ言葉を使った英文を、辞書や新聞、ネットなどで探して書き出してみましょう。

- _____

_____

- _____

_____

Chapter 5

The Tiny House Movement

持続可能な暮らし方

Aim

Transition Words & Phrases for SUMMARY:

[A] in brief（手短に言えば）[A] in other words（言い換えれば）[A] accordingly（そのために）[B] in short（つまり）[L] as a result（結果として）

Core Idea: sustainable living

WARM-UP

それぞれの語句に合う日本語を選んで、記号を（　）に入れましょう。

1. [A] tiny （　　　）　　　　2. [A] core concept （　　　）　3. [A] decrease （　　　）

4. [A] impact （　　　）　　　5. [A] electricity （　　　）　6. [B] location （　　　）

7. [B] public utility （　　　）　8. [B] installation （　　　）　9. [B] food waste （　　　）

10. [L] eco-friendly （　　　）

a. 中心概念	b. 環境にやさしい	c. を減らす	d. 生ごみ	e. 小さな
f. 公共施設	g. 場所	h. 設置	i. 電気	j. 影響

Model Reading A

 18

The tiny house movement is an increasingly popular lifestyle with people today as a sustainable living practice. In brief, the core concepts of the tiny house movement are to live in spaces under 37 square meters, reconnect with nature and live in a climate-conscious manner. In other words, the tiny house movement is one way to lower their

5 cost of living, decrease the impact of human development on nature, and address climate change. Accordingly, all tiny houses are designed to have solar panels, wood stoves, composting toilets, and rainwater collection systems. These systems allow people to live sustainably without city-provided electricity, water, or sewage.

Notes ┈┈┈
sustainable living 持続可能な生き方、地球にやさしい暮らし方 **wood stove** まきストーブ **composting toilet** コンポスト［堆肥化］トイレ **city-provided** 市が提供する **sewage** 下水

I 本文を読んで、下線部に入るもっとも適切なものを a 〜 d より選びましょう。

The tiny house movement is becoming increasingly popular as a means of adopting a _____ lifestyle.

    a. rich   **b.** comfortable   **c.** peaceful   **d.** sustainable

II 本文の内容と一致するように、（   ）に適切な一語を書き入れましょう。

One of the concepts of tiny houses is to live in a way that regains a connection with (   ).

III Model Reading A と同じ内容になるように、次の英文を順に並べ替えましょう。

  1. Putting it another way, this movement helps people live sustainably and cope with climate change.

  2. The tiny house movement is a popular lifestyle for sustainable living.

  3. These systems enable people to live sustainably without relying on public utility services.

  4. Therefore, tiny houses have sustainable systems such as solar panels, wood stoves, composting toilets, and rainwater collection.

  5. In short, it involves living in small spaces and reconnecting with nature.

        (   ) → (   ) → (   ) → (   ) → (   )

Model Reading B

 19

A tiny house is designed to be a complete unit with everything a single person or couple would need. These houses could be parked in nearly any location and set up quickly to provide a modern life without relying on public utilities. With the installation of solar panels and composters designed to break down food waste into gas power, the houses do not need electricity. Wood stoves or small propane heaters produce heat in the winter. Rainwater collection systems gather non-drinkable water for showers and sinks, and composting toilets use no water. In short, tiny houses are designed to be independent of public energy sources by using green technology.

> **Notes** ┈┈┈
> **break down** 分解する **propane heater** プロパンヒーター **energy source** エネルギー源
> **green technology** 環境にやさしい技術

I 本文を読んで、下線部に入るもっとも適切なものを a ～ d より選びましょう。

Rainwater collected for showers and sinks is _____.

    a. also used for cooking   **b.** stored in special tanks

    c. mixed with city-provided water   **d.** not drinkable

II 本文の内容と一致するように、（　　）に適切な一語を書き入れましょう。

The installation of solar panels and biogas power generation have eliminated the need

for (　　　　　　　　　) in tiny houses.

III Reading B と同じ内容になるように、次の英文の下線部に適切な語句を書き入れましょう。

Main Idea: A tiny house is designed as a _____ with everything a person

    or a couple _____.

Supporting Details:

1. These houses can be placed in _____ and offer modern

    living without _____.

2. With _____ and _____ that turn food waste into gas, electricity is

    _____.

3. In the winter, _____ or _____ keep the house warm.

4. Rainwater collection systems gather _____, and composting

    toilets use _____.

Conclusion: This means that tiny houses are designed to use _____

    and avoid dependence on _____.

Ⅳ Reading A と Reading B にそれぞれ適したタイトルを英語で書きましょう。

Reading A : _____

Reading B : _____

LISTENING SECTION

CD 20、21

Ⅰ 次の会話文を聞いて空欄を埋めましょう。

A: Did you hear we started constructing our new tiny house?

B: I heard that! Did you (¹   ) a company to build it?

A: The house is so simple, I didn't have to. As a (²   ), most people can save money and build it themselves. It is much more affordable that way.

B: Why did you (³   ) a tiny house over a conventional one?

A: Tiny houses cost much less than (⁴   ) ones, and I wanted to live in an eco-friendly way. Having a small house means I have less of a carbon footprint.

B: I have heard many are built on trailers. Will your house be (⁵   )?

A: It is built on a trailer. I travel a great deal, and now I can take my house. In (⁶   ) words, having a tiny house will make traveling cheaper and more comfortable.

Notes ....
affordable 無理なく買える **carbon footprint** カーボン・フットプリント（ライフサイクル全体で排出される温室効果ガスの排出量を **CO2** の排出量に換算した指標）

Ⅱ 質問を聞いて、a ～ c のなかから正しい答えを選びましょう。

1. a   b   c

2. a   b   c

WRITING SECTION

✔ 「要約」するつなぎ言葉をうまく使うためのヒント

結論や本当に言いたかったことを導くときに、締めくくりとして「要約」のつなぎ言葉を用います。段落、議論、文章を締めくくるためのつなぎ言葉です。また、アイデアを要約したり、言い直したりする場合にも使われます。

本文で取り上げた以外に、次のような「要約」するつなぎ言葉があります。

all things considered（あらゆることを考えてみると）**as a final note**（締めくくりとして）**as discussed previously**（前に述べたように）**as mentioned above**（上述のように）**finally/lastly**（最後に）**hence**（このような訳で）**in conclusion**（最後に、結論として）**in summary**（要約すると、要するに）**overall**（全体としては、全体的に言えば、概して）**taking everything into consideration**（すべてを考慮すると）**to conclude**（[文頭で]結論から言うと）**to sum up**（要するに、要約すれば）

「要約」するつなぎ言葉の具体的な使い方をみてみましょう。

1. **Finally**, I would like to share my views.
   （**最後に**、私の意見を述べさせていただきます）

   締めくくりの表現としての「最後に」には、これ以外にも、**in closing, last of all, at the end** なども使えます。互換性があるため、いろいろなバリエーションを身につけておくと便利です。

2. **In conclusion**, I submit that the proposal will not work without some minor changes.
   （**結論としては**、この提案は若干の変更を加えなければ機能しないことを提言します）

3. **As a final note**, be sure to read the manual carefully before starting work.
   （**最後に注意点として**、作業を始める前に必ずマニュアルをよく読んでください）

   分詞構文を使った次のような言い方も、定型表現として覚えておきましょう。

4. **All things considered**, we are in the wrong time to start a business.
   （**どう考えても**、今はビジネスを始めるには時期が悪い）

5. **Taking everything into consideration**, this event was a great success.
   （**すべてを考慮すると**、このイベントは大成功だった）

要約は短く、しかも分かりやすく！

結論をまとめるときのつなぎ言葉は、情報記事や論説文、スピーチなどで使用しますが、要約や主張の最終的なポイントを読者や聞き手に伝えるのに効果的です。はっきりと簡潔に述べることが大事です。決まった言い方をしっかり習得しましょう。

Ⅰ 次のそれぞれの英文にもっとも適したつなぎ言葉を下の選択肢から選びましょう。文頭に来る語は大文字で書き始めましょう。

1. In (   ), the following three points can be concluded.

2. (   ), further discussion is a waste of time.

3. Taking everything into (   ), this job offer is my best option.

4. I always check the spelling (   ) to make sure there are no typos.

---

to conclude,   consideration,   at the end,   overall,   summary,
considered

Ⅱ 与えられた語句を使って、次の日本語を英語にしましょう。

1. どう考えても、今はビジネスを始めるには時期が悪い。(all things considered)

_____

_____

2. 結論から言うと、この問題に対する取り組み方は次の３つに集約されます。
(to sum up, tackle)

_____

3. 最後に、私の考えを簡潔に要約したいと思います。(as a final note, summarize)

_____

Ⅲ Let's practice transitions!

例文にならって、文を作ってみましょう。

例文

1. (a) The core concepts of the tiny house movement are to live in a climate-conscious manner.

   (b) **In other words**, people feel that the tiny house movement is one way to address climate change.

Your original

(a) _____

(b) **In other words**, _____

2. (a) The tiny house movement is one way to lower their cost of living and address climate change.

   (b) **Accordingly**, all tiny houses are designed to have solar panels, wood stoves, composting toilets, and rainwater collection systems.

Your original

(a) _____

(b) **Accordingly**, _____

3. (a) Rainwater collection systems gather non-drinkable water for showers and sinks, and composting toilets use no water.

   (b) **In short**, tiny houses are designed to be independent of public energy sources by using green technology.

Your original

(a) _____

(b) **In short**, _____

Ⅳ Finishing Touches for Chapter 5

次のテーマで一つのパラグラフを英文で書きましょう。

テーマ：タイニーハウスに住むというライフスタイルについて

条　件：パラグラフライティングの手法を用いて書く。2つ以上の「要約」のつなぎ言葉を用いる。単語数は100 words 程度とする。

このチャプターでは "tiny house" を通して環境に配慮した生き方を提示しました。あなたはタイニーハウスに住んでみたいと思いますか？　タイニーハウスに住むことのメリット・デメリット、タイニーハウスに住むライフスタイルなどについて、あなたの考えを1つのパラグラフにまとめてみましょう。出来上がったら、文書または口頭で発表しましょう。

Paragraph Title: _____

Introduction Sentence: _____

_____

Supporting Sentences: _____

_____

_____

_____

Concluding Sentence: _____

_____

他にもこんな「要約」のつなぎ言葉があります。

as a consequence of（〜の結果）**consequently**（前述の理由により）**on the whole**（全体的に見ると）**to put it briefly**（手短に言えば）

Brush-up Assignment
「要約」のつなぎ言葉を使った英文を、辞書や新聞、ネットなどで探して書き出してみましょう。

- _____

_____

- _____

_____

Chapter 6

Pervious Concrete

水はけのよいコンクリート

Aim

Transition Words & Phrases for CONTRAST

[A] instead of（の代わりに）[B] rather than（よりはむしろ）[B] on the other hand（他方では）

[B] nevertheless（それにもかかわらず）[L] in contrast to（と対照的に）

Core Idea: natural disaster preparedness

WARM-UP

それぞれの語句に合う日本語を選んで、記号を（　）に入れましょう。

1. [A] pour into (　　) **2.** [A] take advantage of (　　) **3.** [A] natural disaster (　　)

4. [A] enhance (　　) **5.** [B] intentional (　　) **6.** [B] absorb (　　)

7. [B] appropriate (　　) **8.** [B] shed (　　) **9.** [L] excessive (　　)

10. [L] drainage system (　　)

---

a. 意図された　　　b. 自然災害　　　c. を流す　　　d. を上手く生かす　　　e. 排水溝

f. 過剰な　　　g. を高める　　　h. に流し込む　　　i. ふさわしい　　　j. を吸収する

READING SECTION

Model Reading A

Concrete is used in a variety of situations to keep people safe. Concrete is known worldwide as a building material, but it is also a versatile substance that can be easily adapted to any shape and poured into unexpected forms. One type of concrete that takes advantage of these characteristics is pervious concrete. Pervious concrete allows water to flow easily and snow to melt quickly instead of pooling and creating hazards. Regions hit by typhoons, floods, and other natural disasters can use pervious concrete to enhance safety. Pervious concrete is just one example of how concrete is utilized in various applications to protect the security of our lives.

Notes ··
versatile substance 用途の広い物質 **pervious concrete** 浸透性コンクリート

Ⅰ 本文を読んで、下線部に入るもっとも適切なものをa～dより選びましょう。

Concrete is one of the most popular _____ in the world.

　　a. professions　　**b.** stones　　**c.** building materials　　**d.** drainage areas

Ⅱ 本文の内容と一致するように、(　　) に適切な一語を書き入れましょう。

In areas where natural hazards are common, pervious concrete can contribute to (　　　　) conditions.

Ⅲ Model Reading A と同じ内容になるように、次の英文を順に並べ替えましょう。

1. One type of concrete that utilizes this property is pervious concrete.

2. It is a common substance that can be easily adapted anywhere.

3. In this way, concrete is applied in various ways to protect our lives.

4. Concrete is used in a large variety of situations to keep people safe.

5. Pervious concrete can provide safety in areas where water or snow creates hazardous conditions or in places hit by natural disasters.

　　　　(　　) → (　　) → (　　) → (　　) → (　　)

Model Reading B

 23

Pervious concrete has intentional holes to absorb and channel water rather than repel it. Consequently, pervious concrete absorbs water from rain and snow and sends it from the surface into waterways. Removing surface water during a storm can significantly reduce damage to people and places. On the other hand, pervious concrete is much weaker than other forms of concrete because it is full of holes. As a result, it is not an appropriate material for buildings or roads. Nevertheless, its ability to shed water quickly makes it an ideal medium for pedestrian areas in disaster-prone sites, such as parking lots, parks, sidewalks, and carports.

Notes ·········· **repel** ～をはじく **pedestrian area** 歩行者用の場所　**disaster-prone site** 災害多発地域

Ⅰ 本文を読んで、下線部に入るもっとも適切なものを a ～ d より選びましょう。

Pervious concrete is designed with holes to _____.

　　a. absorb water　**b.** repel water　**c.** avoid regular storms　**d.** strengthen buildings

Ⅱ 本文の内容と一致するように、（　　）に適切な一語を書き入れましょう。

Pervious concrete is also suitable for parking lots, sidewalks, and other areas used by many (　　　　　　).

Ⅲ Model Reading B と同じ内容になるように、次の英文の下線部に適切な語句を書き入れましょう。

Main Idea: Pervious concrete is intentionally designed to _____ through _____.

Supporting Details:

1. It captures water from _____ and moves it from _____ into _____.

2. This function can significantly reduce _____ during storms by _____.

3. However, pervious concrete is _____ than _____ because it is _____.

4. As such, it is unsuitable for _____.

Conclusion: Despite this, it is _____ for pedestrians _____ _____ because of its ability to _____ quickly.

Ⅳ Reading A と Reading B にそれぞれ適したタイトルを英語で書きましょう。

Reading A : _____

Reading B : _____

LISTENING SECTION　〉〉

CD 24、25

Ⅰ 次の会話文を聞いて空欄を埋めましょう。

A: Water is essential, but too much water can cause problems like flooding.

B: (^{1}　　　　　　), few people think about how we can manage excessive water.

A: Doesn't too much water just go into the drainage (^{2}　　　　　)?

B: Yes, but using materials such as pervious concrete can (^{3}　　　　　) flood safety.

A: How does pervious concrete work?

B: (^{4}　　　　　) than push water to the drain, it absorbs water directly and drains in a (^{5}　　　　　) way.

A: I see! So pervious concrete helps rain and stormwater be absorbed evenly?

B: Exactly! In (^{6}　　　　　) to normal drainage, pervious concrete can keep water channels clear and prevent flooding.

Ⅱ 質問を聞いて、正しい答えを a 〜 c から選びましょう。

1. a　　b　　c

2. a　　b　　c

WRITING SECTION

> ✔ **「対比」に関するつなぎ言葉をうまく使うためのヒント**
>
> 「対比」を表すつなぎ言葉は、先に述べられたことと対照的に、違う考えや状況を提示するときに用います。直前の内容について、別の視点での見方や意見を述べるときに対比を表すつなぎ言葉を使うことは、考えや相反する意見を明確にする上でとても大事な役目を果たします。

本文で出てきた以外に、次のような「対比」のつなぎ言葉があります。

alternatively（その代わりに）**by/in contrast**（一方）**in contrast to**（と比べると）**instead**（その代わりに）**on the contrary**（それどころか、逆に）**on the other hand**（一方で）**while this may be true**（これは本当かもしれないが）

「対比」に関するつなぎ言葉の具体的な使い方をみてみましょう。

■ 混同しがちな「にもかかわらず」の表現

despite: 品詞は前置詞です。後には名詞がきます。（× despite of）

in spite of: 3つの語で一つの前置詞を形成します。後には名詞がきます。

despite the fact that: **that** の後には節（S + V）がきます。

in spite of the fact that: **that** の後には節（S + V）がきます。

1. **Despite** his busy schedule, Tom spends his weekends volunteering.
   （多忙な日々を送っている**にもかかわらず**、トムは週末をボランティア活動に費やしている）

2. I performed well in front of the audience **in spite of** my lack of preparation.
   （準備不足**にもかかわらず**、観客の前で良いパフォーマンスができた）

■ 「それにもかかわらず」を表す **nonetheless**, **nevertheless**, **notwithstanding** は、いずれも複合語 (compound words) で、(none + the + less, never + the + less, not + withstand + ing) から成り立っています。よく似ていますが、品詞と意味を点検しておきましょう。

nonetheless と **nevertheless** はどちらも「副詞」で、意味はほぼ同じです。
一方、**notwithstanding** には、前置詞で使われる場合と**副詞**で使われる場合があります。

3. **Notwithstanding** his lack of experience, he was given the job because of his excellent skills.（前置詞 =**despite**）
   （未経験**ながら**、彼の優れた技術が評価され、仕事を任されることになった。）

4. I attended class, **notwithstanding** feeling unwell.（副詞 = **regardless of**）
   （体調が悪い**にもかかわらず**、授業に出席した）

nonetheless, **nevertheless**, **notwithstanding** の3語は、nonetheless → nevertheless → notwithstanding の順にフォーマルな印象が増します。書くときに使用頻度が高いのは **nevertheless** です。話し言葉としては、これらの同意語の **however** を使うのが一般的です。

I 次のそれぞれの英文にもっとも適切なつなぎ言葉を下の選択肢から選びましょう。

1. She went for a run in the park (   ) heavy rain was about to fall.

2. I forgot my umbrella this morning; (   ), I didn't get too wet because the rain was very light.

3. I thought he would be upset by the news, but (   ), he seemed quite pleased about it.

4. Taking the bus is longer, but (   ), you can make time to read during the ride.

in spite of,   on the other hand,   on the contrary,   in contrast,
despite the fact that,   nonetheless

II 与えられた語句を使って、次の日本語を英語にしましょう。

1. 昨日の晴天とは打って変わって、今日は曇り空で肌寒く感じる。(in contrast to, chilly)

_____

2. 私の片言の英語にもかかわらず、彼らは私の言いたいことをわかってくれた。
(despite, broken English)

_____

3. 確かにそうかもしれませんが、問題は、そうすることであなたの尊厳を傷つけているのかもしれない、ということです。(while this may be true, offending, dignity)

_____

Ⅲ Let's practice transitions!

例文にならって、文を作ってみましょう。

例文

1. Pervious concrete allows water to flow easily and snow to melt quickly **instead of** pooling and creating water hazards.

Your original

_____

instead of _____

2. Pervious concrete has intentional holes to absorb and channel water **rather than** repelling it.

Your original

_____

rather than _____

3. (a) It is not an appropriate material for buildings or roads.

(b) **Nevertheless**, its ability to shed water quickly makes it an ideal medium for pedestrian areas.

Your original

(a) _____

(b) **Nevertheless,** _____

次のテーマで一つのパラグラフを英文で書きましょう。

> **テーマ**：＿＿＿（という自然災害）に対して私がしている対策
>
> **条　件**：パラグラフライティングの手法を用いて書く。2つ以上の「対比」のつなぎ言葉を用いる。単語数は 100 words 程度とする。

日本では自然災害がよく起きます。大きな災害を防ぐために、私たちにはどんなことができるでしょうか。地震、津波、台風などの自然災害に対して、あなたがしている対策や、取り組みたいことを主題にして、1つのパラグラフにまとめてみましょう。出来上がったら、文書または口頭で発表しましょう。

Paragraph Title: ＿＿＿＿＿＿＿＿＿＿＿＿＿＿＿＿＿＿

Introduction Sentence: ＿＿＿＿＿＿＿＿＿＿＿＿＿＿

＿＿＿＿＿＿＿＿＿＿＿＿＿＿＿＿＿＿＿＿＿＿＿＿＿

Supporting Sentences: ＿＿＿＿＿＿＿＿＿＿＿＿＿＿＿

＿＿＿＿＿＿＿＿＿＿＿＿＿＿＿＿＿＿＿＿＿＿＿＿＿

＿＿＿＿＿＿＿＿＿＿＿＿＿＿＿＿＿＿＿＿＿＿＿＿＿

Concluding Sentence: ＿＿＿＿＿＿＿＿＿＿＿＿＿＿＿

＿＿＿＿＿＿＿＿＿＿＿＿＿＿＿＿＿＿＿＿＿＿＿＿＿

他にもこんな「対比」のつなぎ言葉があります。

although（〜ではあるが）**although this may be true / this may be true but**（これは本当かもしれないが）**by contrast with**（と対照的に）**contrarily**（これに反して）**conversely**（逆に言うと、反対に）**even though**（〜であるけれども）**that said**（[文頭で] そうは言っても）**unlike**（[前置詞] 〜とは異なって）**while**（[接続詞] しかし一方）**while on the contrary**（それに対して）**yet**（[接続詞] だがそれでも）

Brush-up Assignment
「対比」のつなぎ言葉を使った英文を、辞書や新聞、ネットなどで探して書き出してみましょう。

- ＿＿＿＿＿＿＿＿＿＿＿＿＿＿＿＿＿＿＿＿＿＿＿＿

＿＿＿＿＿＿＿＿＿＿＿＿＿＿＿＿＿＿＿＿＿＿＿＿＿

- ＿＿＿＿＿＿＿＿＿＿＿＿＿＿＿＿＿＿＿＿＿＿＿＿

＿＿＿＿＿＿＿＿＿＿＿＿＿＿＿＿＿＿＿＿＿＿＿＿＿

Chapter 7

Melt in Your Mouth!

アメリカの伝統的なお菓子

Aim

Transition Words & Phrases for EMPHASIS:

[A] of course（もちろん）[A] in truth（実は）[B] above all（そして何より）[B] truly（まさに）[L] really（本当に）[L] undoubtedly（明らかに）

Core Idea: global sweets

○ WARM-UP ○

それぞれの語句に合う日本語を選んで、記号を（　）に入れましょう。

1. [A] connect with（　　）　**2.** [A] age-old（　　）　**3.** [A] confection（　　）

4. [A] heritage（　　）　**5.** [B] founder（　　）　**6.** [B] available（　　）　**7.** [B] slogan（　　）

8. [B] favorite（　　）　**9.** [L] flavor（　　）　**10.** [L] sticky（　　）

> a. 風味　　b. お気に入りの　　c. 昔からある　　d. 〜と結びつける　　e. 手に入る
>
> f. べたべたした　　g. 創始者　　h. お菓子　　i. 宣伝文句　　j. 遺産

Model Reading A

 26

In a global world, sweets are one of the ways we connect with other cultures. Each country has its traditional sweets, from Japan's age-old daifuku and kashiwa-mochi to French cream brulé. Of course, America also has several conventional confections, the most famous being M&Ms, which are small round chocolates coated with hard candy
5   shells. In truth, the creator of M&Ms, Forrest Mars, Sr., got the idea during the Spanish Civil War when he saw soldiers eating small chocolates with a hard sugar coating to prevent melting. Today, M&Ms are cultural icons, spreading American heritage around the world through chocolate.

Notes ··
cream brulé クレームブリュレ（クリームブリュレ）**Forrest Mars, Sr.** フォレスト・マーズ・シニア
(1904–99) cultural icon 文化の象徴 **M&Ms** の表記に関しては **M&M's** もあるが、本書では **M&Ms**
を採用している。**M&Ms** という名称は、会社ではなく実際のキャンディそのものを指す。会社を指す場合
は、**Mars, Inc** または **Mars Candy Company** と表記する。

Ⅰ 本文を読んで、下線部に入るもっとも適切なものを a ～ d より選びましょう。

The small chocolates the soldiers were eating had hard sugar on them, so the candies
_____.

    a. were very sweet   **b.** melted immediately   **c.** did not melt
    d. tasted strange

Ⅱ 本文の内容と一致するように、（　　）に適切な一語を書き入れましょう。

Forrest Mars, Sr. later became the (　　　　　) of M&Ms.

Ⅲ Model Reading A と同じ内容になるように、次の英文を順に並べ替えましょう。

1. Every country also has its own traditional sweets.

2. Sweets serve as a medium to connect with other cultures today.

3. Naturally, America as well has several traditional sweets, the most famous being M&Ms.

4. Nowadays, M&Ms have played an important role in spreading American traditions around the world through chocolate.

5. In fact, M&Ms were inspired when Forrest Mars, Sr. saw soldiers in Spain eating hard sugar-coated chocolate.

        （　　）→（　　）→（　　）→（　　）→（　　）

Model Reading B

Here is a brief history of M&Ms. M&M stands for Forrest Mars and Bruce Murrie, the company's two founders. They aimed, above all, to create a lightweight candy that couldn't melt in extreme heat. The candies were first released to the U.S. military in 1941. They became publicly available after the war, and the American tradition of M&Ms truly began. The slogan "Melt in your mouth, not in your hands" was created by the Mars Candy Company and used to advertise M&Ms beginning in 1954. Since then, the slogan has become a synonym for the M&Ms brand. M&Ms quickly gained global popularity and are now a favorite candy worldwide.

....

Notes   **Bruce Murrie** ブルース・ムリー **(1909–78)**   **lightweight** 軽量の "**Melt in your mouth, not in your hands**"「お口でとろけて、手にとけない」**synonym** 同意語

Ⅰ 本文を読んで、下線部に入るもっとも適切なものを a ～ d より選びましょう。

The slogan "Melt in your mouth, not in your hands" has become a _____ of the M&Ms brand.

    a. flavor   **b.** competitor   **c.** symbol   **d.** color

Ⅱ 本文の内容と一致するように、( ) に適切な一語を書き入れましょう。

The candy was first released in 1941 for the U.S. military and became available to the ( ) after the war.

Ⅲ Model Reading B と同じ内容になるように、次の英文の下線部に適切な語句を書き入れましょう。

Main Idea: M&M's history started with two people, _____ and _____.

Supporting Details:

1. They wanted to make a candy that was light and wouldn't _____.

2. The U.S. _____ was the first to receive these candies in _____.

3. After the war, M&Ms became widely sold to ordinary people, beginning the _____ in the United States.

4. Since 1954, when their _____ was launched, the slogan "Melt in your _____, not in your _____" has been associated with the M&Ms brand.

Conclusion: M&Ms quickly became _____ and are now the world's _____.

Ⅳ Reading A と Reading B にそれぞれ適したタイトルを英語で書きましょう。

Reading A : _____

Reading B : _____

LISTENING SECTION ≫

Ⅰ 次の会話文を聞いて空欄を埋めましょう。

A: I've always loved M&Ms. They are such a (**1** _____) American candy.

B: Yeah, I love how they come in so many different colors and flavors.

A: (**2** _____); it's cool they have seasonal flavors like peppermint for Christmas and pumpkin pie in the fall.

B: It's like how traditional Japanese confections (**3** _____) depending on the season.

A: I agree. What I also love about M&Ms is that we can put them on ice cream or bake them into (**4** _____).

B: Yeah, and I really like the slogan "Melt in your mouth, not in your hands."

A: It's true. You can enjoy the (**5** _____) without getting your fingers sticky.

B: And it's (**6** _____) they've expanded to 86 countries with 57 flavors. They're undoubtedly a worldwide favorite.

Ⅱ 質問を聞いて、正しい答えを a ～ c から選びましょう。

1. a   b   c

2. a   b   c

WRITING SECTION

✔ 「強調」に関するつなぎ言葉をうまく使うためのヒント

強調のつなぎ言葉は、ある事柄の重要性を印象づけたり、特に主張を強調して提示するときに使用します。これらのつなぎ言葉は、文章でも話し言葉でも使用でき、メッセージをより明確に、よりインパクトのあるものにする際に役立ちます。

本文で取り上げた以外に、次のような「強調」に関するつなぎ言葉があります。
above all（そして何より）**in particular**（特に、とりわけ）**of course**（もちろん）**without a doubt**（確実に、間違いなく）他に -ly のついた副詞が多数あります。

-ly のついた副詞で「強調」するつなぎ言葉の具体的な使い方をみてみましょう。

1. The success of this project is **chiefly/largely/mainly/primarily** due to the cooperation of all of you.

   （このプロジェクトが成功したのは、主としてみなさんの協力のおかげです）

chiefly, **largely**, **mainly**, **primarily** は、「主として」という意味で使うときには、互換性があります。

2. His skills in English are excellent, **especially** in his English compositions.

   （彼の英語力は卓越しているが、とりわけ英作文のスキルは素晴らしい）

3. Everyone in this class is good at sports, but Kenta **particularly** is an all-around athlete.

   （このクラスはみんなスポーツが得意だが、特にケンタは何でもできる）

especially, **particularly** は「なかでも特に、とりわけ〜」という意味で、何かを強調したい時に使うときにespecially やparticularly を同じように使います。修飾したい語の直前に置きますが、主語を修飾したい時は主語の直後に置きます。

4. My grades **significantly** improved after I started studying with her.

   （彼女と一緒に勉強するようになってから、成績が著しく上がった）

significantly（大いに、著しく）は increase, rise, go up などと一緒に、変化が劇的に変わる様子を表すときに使います。文中や文尾で使われます。

5. The company's customer base is **overwhelmingly** young people.

   （同社の顧客層は圧倒的に若者が多い）

動詞の overwhelm は「（数の多さで）〜を圧倒する、（感情が）打ちのめす」という意味なので、**overwhelmingly** は「圧倒的に、圧倒的多数で」という意味合いで使います。

I 次のそれぞれの英文にもっとも適切なつなぎ言葉を下の選択肢から選びましょう。

1. In Japan, the birth rate has declined (   ).

2. We talked for hours, but (   ) he disagrees with me.

3. I thought I had lost my cell phone, but (   ), I had left it in my friend's room.

4. The meeting was supposed to continue for a long time; (   ), it lasted for more than two hours.

> even now,   of course,   actually,   basically,   significantly,   indeed,

II 与えられた語句を使って、次の日本語を英語にしましょう。

1. オリビアは異文化を学ぶことに興味があるが、なかでも日本文化に魅了されている。
(Olivia, fascinated, in particular)

_____

_____

2. 私のレポートはよい出来だとは思わなかったが、実際のところ、合格すれすれだった。
(in truth, barely passed)

_____

_____

3. 彼のプレゼンテーションは分かりやすい。その上、同意する点が多い。(besides)

_____

_____

Ⅲ Let's practice transitions!

例文にならって、文を作ってみましょう。

例文

1. (a) Each country has its traditional sweets.

   (b) **Of course**, America also has several traditional candies, the most famous
   being M&Ms.

Your original

   (a) _____

   (b) **Of course**, _____

2. They aimed, **above all**, to create a lightweight candy that couldn't melt in
   extreme heat.

Your original

   _____, **above all**, _____

3. M&Ms are **undoubtedly** a worldwide favorite.

Your original

   _____ **undoubtedly** _____

IV Finishing Touches for Chapter 7

次のテーマで一つのパラグラフを英文で書きましょう。

> **テーマ**：私が好きなお菓子
>
> **条　件**：パラグラフライティングの手法を用いて書く。2つ以上の「強調」するつなぎ言葉を用いる。単語数は 100 words 程度とする。

本文では、アメリカの伝統的なお菓子である M&Ms の歴史が述べられています。世界にはさまざまな伝統のあるお菓子類がありますが、その中で、日本を含むどの国や地域のものでもいいので、あなたが好きなお菓子を一つ取り上げて、1つのパラグラフにまとめてみましょう。出来上がったら、文書または口頭で発表しましょう。

Paragraph Title: _____

Introduction Sentence: _____

_____

Supporting Sentences: _____

_____

_____

_____

Concluding Sentence: _____

_____

他にもこんな「強調」するつなぎ言葉があります。

absolutely（まったく）**actually**（実際は）**certainly**（確かに）**clearly**（明らかに）**in essence**（本質的に）**surprisingly**（驚いたことに）**unquestionably**（紛れもなく）

Brush-up Assignment

「強調」するつなぎ言葉を使った英文を、辞書や新聞、ネットなどで探して書き出してみましょう。

- _____

  _____

- _____

  _____

Chapter 8

The Story of Peanuts

チャーリー・ブラウンと仲間たち

Aim

Transition Words & Phrases for CONCESSION:

[A] although（〜であるけれども）[A] despite（にもかかわらず：in spite of より堅い語）[B] while it may be true（それは本当かもしれないが）[B] in spite of（にもかかわらず）

Core Idea: the value of comics and cartoons

WARM-UP

それぞれの語に合う日本語を選んで、記号を（　）に入れましょう。

1. [A] anxiety (　　　)　**2.** [A] amusing (　　　)　**3.** [A] premise (　　　)　**4.** [A] humane (　　　)

5. [B] renowned (　　)　**6.** [B] incredibly (　　　)　**7.** [B] sincere (　　　)　**8.** [B] relate to (　　　)

9. [B] misfortune (　　　)　**10.** [B] foundation (　　　)

a. 人間味のある	b. 不安	c. 根幹	d. 有名な	e. 誠実な	f. に共感する
g. 不運	h. 前提	i. 面白い	j. 信じられないほど		

READING SECTION

Model Reading A

 30

       Childhood is an exciting time, full of wonder and joy, and at the same time, filled with anxiety and stress. Although this may not seem particularly amusing, it's the premise of the comic strip *Peanuts* by Charles M. Schulz. The strip stars a group of neighborhood children with unique interests, challenges, and skills. The children often learn lessons by
5 struggling to overcome their challenges. Despite having such a serious theme, the strips are hilarious because the characters are relatable and humane. By focusing on the lighter side of childhood, *Peanuts* became America's favorite comic strip.

Notes　star〔動詞〕を主役にする **Charles M. Schulz** チャールズ・モンロー・シュルツ、アメリカの漫画家（**1922 –2000**）**comic strip**〔新聞などに掲載される〕続き漫画、コミック・ストリップ（新聞の連載漫画で，横長の帯 [ストリップ] 状に掲載されていることから）**hilarious** 実に愉快な **relatable** 親しみやすい

I 本文を読んで、下線部に入るもっとも適切なものを a ～ d より選びましょう。

Peanuts is America's longest-running _____.

    a. television show   **b.** movie series

    c. comic strip   **d.** agricultural product

II 本文の内容と一致するように、（　　）に適切な一語を書き入れましょう。

（　　　　　　　　　） the serious subject matter, *Peanuts* is interesting because the characters are familiar and very humane.

III Model Reading A と同じ内容になるように、次の英文を順に並べ替えましょう。

   1. The comic's main characters are neighborhood kids.

   2. *Peanuts* became America's most popular cartoon by emphasizing the bright side of childhood.

   3. Childhood is an exciting time full of wonder, joy, anxiety, and stress.

   4. The comic shows these characters struggling with weaknesses and trying to overcome them.

   5. This is the underlying premise of comic strip *Peanuts* by Charles M. Schulz.

        （　　）→（　　）→（　　）→（　　）→（　　）

Model Reading B

 31

Peanuts debuted in American newspapers in 1950 and ran without hiatus until Schulz died in 2000. Many characters became internationally famous, such as Linus, Lucy, Woodstock, Charlie Brown, and Snoopy, fiction's most renowned beagle! While it may be true that every character is somebody's favorite, the stories often focus on the incredibly unlucky Charlie Brown. Charlie is a sincere boy who wants to do well and tries hard at everything but generally fails. In spite of his poor luck, readers relate to Charlie Brown because he never gives up, despite his countless failures. Charlie's misfortune is the foundation of *Peanuts* and has captivated generations of readers.

Notes ....
debut 初登場（デビュー）する **ran without hiatus** 休むことなく連載された **beagle** ビーグル犬
captivate 魅了する

Ⅰ 本文を読んで、下線部に入るもっとも適切なものを a 〜 d より選びましょう。

The following statement regarding Charlie Brown is incorrect: _____
- **a.** Charlie is an unbelievably unlucky boy.
- **b.** Charlie is an honest boy.
- **c.** Charlie is usually successful in whatever he does.
- **d.** Charlie fails repeatedly, but he never gives up.

Ⅱ 本文の内容と一致するように、（　　）に適切な一語を書き入れましょう。

Among the many characters in *Peanuts*, (   ), the beagle dog, has also become world-famous.

Ⅲ Model Reading B と同じ内容になるように、次の英文の下線部に適切な語句を書きましょう。

Main Idea: Charles Schulz's *Peanuts* appeared in _____ from _____ until _____.

Supporting Details:

1. The comic strip produced _____, such as _____ _____.

2. The character most often associated with *Peanuts* is _____.

3. Readers empathize with Charlie Brown, who never _____ no matter how much he _____.

Conclusion: Charlie's _____ is at the heart of *Peanuts* and has fascinated many _____ of readers.

IV Reading A と Reading B にそれぞれ適したタイトルを英語で書きましょう。

Reading A : _____

Reading B : _____

LISTENING SECTION

CD 32、33

I 次の会話文を聞いて空欄を埋めましょう。

A: Do you have a favorite comic strip?

B: Yes! My favorite comic strip is *Peanuts*, by Charles Schulz.

A: Mine, too! I have (^{1}) loved Snoopy, but I stopped reading them when I was a kid. Are they still (^{2}) the series?

B: No, the strip ended with Schulz's death in 2000. (^{3}) his death, they still make new movies and video games.

A: Wow! It's amazing there is still new material for something that (^{4}) in 2000.

B: The strip ran for 50 years, so there were lots of things (^{5}) people could adapt into movies and games, even without new comics.

A: I had no idea *Peanuts* ran for 50 years!

B: It's true. Schulz wrote (^{6}) 18,000 strips in total, so new readers can enjoy generations of comics.

II 質問を聞いて、a 〜 c のなかから正しい答えを選びましょう。

1. a   b   c

2. a   b   c

WRITING SECTION

✔ 「譲歩」のつなぎ言葉をうまく使うためのヒント

concession（譲歩）とは、concede（しぶしぶ認める）という動詞の名詞形です。
前の部分に対して、「それなのに」と付け加えたり、同意しながらも別の意見を述べたり、他の考えに歩み寄って「〜だけれども」「たとえ〜だとしても」と言いたいときに使います。譲歩のつなぎ言葉は、主旨と異なる、あるいは反対するポイントを紹介したり、反対意見を認めたり、議論や討論を続ける前に一点を認めたりするのに使用されます。

本文で取り上げた以外では、次のような「譲歩」を表すつなぎ言葉があります。
although it may be so（そうかもしれないが）**at any rate**（いずれにしても）**even if/though**（仮定の話として、たとえ〜だとしても）**granted (that)**（仮に〜だとしても）**regardless of**（〜にかかわらず）**though**（[接続詞] 〜であるけれども：although より口語的）

「譲歩」を表すつなぎ言葉の具体的な使い方をみてみましょう。

1. **Even if** you ask me repeatedly, I would not accept it.
   （**たとえ**何度お願いされて**も**、お断りします）

   Even if を文中に用いて、I would not accept it, **even if** you ask me repeatedly. のように書くこともできます。
   even if や even though の even は if や though を強調していますが、Even you ask me・・・と、even を単独で使うことはできません。

2. **Granted (that)** I may not pass the exam this time, I will not give up and will take it again.
   （**仮に**今回は合格できなく**ても**、あきらめずにまた受験します）

   granted (that) は過去分詞で始まっている分詞構文で、接続詞的に使われます。that 以下は「仮に・・・」と言っていますが、仮定法は使いません。that はよく省略されます。

3. **However** you try to explain it, I don't quite follow you.
   （どのように説明されて**も**、よく分からない）

4. **Whichever** option you choose, there'll be disadvantages.
   （どちらを選んで**も**、デメリットがあります）

   wh-words (how, what, which, when, where, who) に **-ever** をつけると、「例え〜したとしても」という譲歩の意味を込めて表せます。

wh-words (how, what, which, when, where, who) は、no matter + wh-words で置き換えて言うこともできます。（例：no matter how, no matter what）

Whatever (= No matter what) path you take, you will get there.
（どのような道であっても、必ずたどり着けますよ）

文中に出る **despite**（にもかかわらず）は前置詞なので、次にくるのは名詞か動名詞。in spite of と混同して、of を次にもってきてはいけません。

I 次のそれぞれの英文にもっとも適したつなぎ言葉を下の選択肢から選びましょう。文頭に来る語は大文字で書き始めましょう。

1. (   ) of his busy schedule, he always finds time for his family.

2. Come again (   ) you like.

3. I was exhausted. (   ), I had to finish my assignment.

4. I will not tolerate such prejudice, (   ) says it.

> despite, no matter who, nevertheless, though, whenever, regardless

---

II 与えられた語句を使って、次の日本語を英語にしましょう。

1. たとえこの授業が難しくても、私は途中で投げ出さずに必ずやり遂げます。
   (even though, challenging)

   _____

   _____

2. どこに住んでいても、新しいことに挑戦する機会は常にあります。(wherever)

   _____

   _____

3. 授業にはきちんと出席していたにもかかわらず、期末テストの結果は散々だった。
   (in spite of, attendance)

   _____

   _____

Ⅲ Let's practice transitions!

例文にならって、文を作ってみましょう。

例文

1. **Although** this may not seem particularly amusing, it's the premise of the comic strip *Peanuts*.

Your original

Although _____

2. **Despite** having such a serious theme, the strips are hilarious because the characters are relatable and humane.

Your original

Despite _____

3. **While it may be true** that every character is somebody's favorite, the stories often focus on the incredibly unlucky Charlie Brown.

Your original

While it may be true _____

_____

次のテーマで一つのパラグラフを英文で書きましょう。

> **テーマ**：私の好きなマンガとその理由
>
> **条　件**：パラグラフライティングの手法を用いて書く。2つ以上の「譲歩」のつなぎ
> 言葉を用いる。単語数は 100 words 程度とする。

Peanuts のマンガでは、失敗続きの人生を送る Charlie Brown に対して、人々は共感をいだき、生きていく希望を見出してきました。そのようなマンガを、あなたも読んだことがありませんか？　今回は、あなたに影響を与えた作品やその作品の魅力、あなたに感銘を与えた登場人物などを取り上げて、1つのパラグラフにまとめてみましょう。出来上がったら、文書または口頭で発表しましょう。

Paragraph Title: _____

Introduction Sentence: _____

_____

Supporting Sentences: _____

_____

_____

Concluding Sentence: _____

_____

他にもこんな「譲歩」のつなぎ言葉があります。

admittedly（明らかに、ご指摘の通り）**be that as it may**（仮にそうだとしても）**for all that**（とは言うものの）**in any case**（いずれにせよ）**still**（それでもやはり）

Brush-up Assignment
「譲歩」をあらわすつなぎ言葉を使った英文を、辞書や新聞、ネットなどで探して書き出してみましょう。

- _____
_____
- _____
_____

The Sport of Horse Dancing – Dressage

馬術というスポーツ

Aim

Transition words & Phrases for GENERALIZING

^A generally（一般的に）^A generally speaking（一般的には）^B commonly（一般的には）

^L ordinarily（通常）^L as a rule（原則的には）

Core Idea: unusual sports

WARM-UP

それぞれの語句に合う日本語を選んで、記号を（　）に入れましょう。

1. ^A numerous (　　) **2.** ^A maze (　　) **3.** ^A sprint (　　) **4.** ^A impressive (　　)

5. ^A competitive (　　) **6.** ^B originate in (　　) **7.** ^B documented (　　)

8. ^B revive (　　) **9.** ^B evolve into (　　) **10.** ^L command (　　)

a. 迷路　　b. に始まる　　c. 印象的な　　d. 命令　　e. へ発展する

f. 文書化された　　g. 数多くの　　h. 全力疾走する　　i. 競争の激しい　　j. 復活させる

Model Reading A

 34

   Compared to the numerous animal sports worldwide, dressage stands out for its uniqueness. When people think of animal sports, they generally think of dogs running through mazes or horses sprinting down a racetrack. These are two common examples of the over 100 animal sports traditions worldwide. There are also unusual animal
5 sports, such as elephant polo and falconry. Among these, dressage, or horse dancing, is a singular, impressive, and strangely attractive sport. Generally speaking, dressage is considered a French sport. It is non-violent and is regarded as so competitive and complex that it has become an Olympic event.

> **Notes** ⋯⋯
> **dressage** ドレッサージュ（馬場馬術）**stand out for** 〜の点で突出している **elephant polo** エレファントポロ（象に乗ってプレーするポロ競技）**falconry** 鷹狩り

Ⅰ 本文を読んで、下線部に入るもっとも適切なものを a 〜 d より選びましょう。

There are many _____ animal sports, one of which is dressage.
     a. extreme   **b.** fun   **c.** difficult   **d.** unusual

Ⅱ 本文の内容と一致するように、（　　）に適切な一語を書き入れましょう。

Dressage, the art of (　　　　　) dancing, stands out for its uniqueness among the numerous animal sports.

Ⅲ Model Reading A と同じ内容になるように、次の英文を順に並べ替えましょう。

   1. Of all these, dressage is an incredibly captivating sport.

   2. It is non-violent and has become an Olympic event due to its competitive and complex nature.

   3. Dressage is one of the animal sports in the world that stands out for being unique.

   4. There are also unusual animal sports, such as elephant polo and falconry.

   5. Common animal sports examples are dog mazes and horse races of more than 100 animal sports.

   （　　）→（　　）→（　　）→（　　）→（　　）

Model Reading B

 35

Dressage originated in ancient Greece as a sophisticated form of military cavalry drills. In general belief, Xenophon wrote the first documented description of dressage around 400 BCE. However, the practice fell out of favor for hundreds of years. It was revived in France in the 1800s and is commonly referred to as "dressage," which means
5   "training" in French, emphasizing the importance of a harmonious partnership between horse and rider. Dressage is now a worldwide sport that highlights human and animal collaboration. Thus, dressage has rich history, dating back to ancient times, and has evolved into the elegant and precise sport we see today.

Notes   **military cavalry drills** 軍隊の騎兵訓練 **BCE (=before the Common Era)** 西暦紀元前 **Xenophon** ク セノフォン（前 **430** 頃 **-354** 頃）古代ギリシアの軍人、著作家 **fall out of favor** 人気が落ちる

Ⅰ 本文を読んで、下線部に入るもっとも適切なものを a～d より選びましょう。

Dressage began as _____ for horses and riders in ancient Greece.
   a. rodeo shows   **b.** military training drills   **c.** game   **d.** parade routines

Ⅱ 本文の内容と一致するように、（   ）に適切な一語を書き入れましょう。

It is (   ) believed that the first written reference to horsemanship was written
by Xenophon around 400 BCE.

Ⅲ Model Reading B と同じ内容になるように、次の英文の下線部に適切な語句を書き入れましょう。

Main Idea: Dressage is a unique way of _____ that began in _____
   for military use.

Supporting Details:

1. The first written description was made around _____ by _____.

2. The practice had declined for _____ but was _____
   in France in the 1800s.

3. In France, it was called "_____," meaning "training," and emphasized
   the relationship between _____ and _____.

4. Dressage is now a _____ that focuses on how well horses and riders
   can _____.

Conclusion: Dressage has a _____ history and is now a sport of _____
   and precision.

IV Reading A と Reading B にそれぞれ適したタイトルを英語で書きましょう。

Reading A : _____

Reading B : _____

LISTENING SECTION ⟩⟩

🎧 CD 36、37

I 次の会話文を聞いて空欄を埋めましょう。

A: My favorite Olympic event is called "dressage." Riders and horses perform
(¹   ) to music.

B: That seems fun but difficult. How do they (²   ) for the event?

A: Well, ordinarily, riders and trainers teach steps and movements to music.

B: What (³   ) of music do the performances use?

A: They can be trained to dance to anything; classical, modern pop, even
(⁴   ) music!

B: How do the riders communicate with the horse? Do they use something like
whistles or words?

A: As a rule, the rider can only use silent commands with their (⁵   ),
legs, and saddle position to tell the horse what to do.

B: (⁶   )! Now I want to watch a performance at the next Olympics.

II 質問を聞いて、正しい答えを a ～ c から選びましょう。

1. a   b   c

2. a   b   c

WRITING SECTION

> ✔ 「一般化」するつなぎ言葉をうまく使うためのヒント
> 「一般化」するつなぎ言葉は、幅広く大まかなことを述べたり、大量の情報を要約したりするのに使われます。「一般化」するとは、あることを全体に適用できるように、特定のケースだけでなく広い範囲をカバーすることを意味します。

本文で取り上げた以外に、次のような「一般化」を表すつなぎ言葉があります。

all in all（全般的に見て）**all things considered**（総合的に考えてみると）**as usual**（いつものように）**basically**（基本的に）**by and large**（総体的に）**in general**（一般的に）**overall**（全体的に言えば）**regularly**（定期的に）**typically**（概して）**without exception**（例外なく）

「一般化」を表すつなぎ言葉の具体的な使い方をみてみましょう。

■「一般に」（commonly, in general）
一般化して言いたいときに、日本語では「一般（的）に」という言い方が広く使われていますが、英語では、generally が代表的な語です。それ以外に in general や commonly などがよく使われます。

1. **In general**, minimum wage increases raise real incomes.
   （**一般的には**、最低賃金の引き上げは実質所得を引き上げる）

2. This is one of the most **commonly** used methods.
   （これはもっとも**一般的に**使われている方法の一つです）

■「総じて」（by and large, on the whole, overall, typically, all in all）
「総じて」は日本語としてはちょっと固い言葉ではありますが、例外は多少あるにしても、「全体の傾向からすると」という意味で使います。

3. **By and large**, everything is proceeding satisfactorily.
   （**おおむね**、すべて順調に進んでいます）

4. My views are the same as yours **on the whole**.
   （私の考えは、**全体的**に皆さんと同じです）

■「たいていの場合」（mostly, for the most part）
「たいていの場合」は、ほとんどすべてに当てはまることを表したい場合に使います。

5. We communicate **mostly** by cell phone.
   （連絡は**ほとんど**携帯電話で行っています）

6. Japanese game consoles are, **for the most part**, of superior quality.
   （日本のゲーム機は、**ほとんどの場合**、品質が優れている）

前のページで取り上げた -ly のついた単語１語で「一般化」を表すつなぎ言葉はすべて「形容詞 + -ly」で副詞になっています。そこで、どの単語を選ぶか迷ったときは、元の形容詞の意味を考え、そこから派生した単語を選びましょう。

Ⅰ 次のそれぞれの英文にもっとも適したつなぎ言葉を下の選択肢から選びましょう。文頭に来る語は大文字で書き始めましょう。

1. I try to exercise (　　　　　　　　　　　　　) to stay fit and healthy.

2. (　　　　　　　　　　), I think the team did a great job on the project.

3. All half-price sales, (　　　　　　　　　　), end tomorrow.

4. (　　　　　　　　　), we just need you to sign this document.

> basically,　　overall,　　for the most part,　　regularly,　　necessarily,
> without exception

Ⅱ 与えられた語句を使って、次の日本語を英語にしましょう。

1. 台風は今日中に通り過ぎる見込みなので、明日は通常通り授業が行われる予定です。
(as usual, pass)

_____

_____

2. 一般的に、運動は身体と精神の両方の健康に良いと言われている。
(generally speaking, exercise)

_____

_____

3. 諸般の事情を考慮すると、会議を来週まで延期したのは正しい判断だったと思う。
(all things considered, postpone)

_____

_____

Ⅲ Let's practice transitions!

例文にならって、文を作ってみましょう。

例文

1. When people think of animal sports, they **generally** think of dogs running through mazes or horses sprinting down a racetrack.

Your original

_____

generally _____

2. Ordinarily, riders and trainers teach steps and movements to music.

Your original

Ordinarily, _____

3. As a rule, the rider can only give instructions to the horse by silent commands.

Your original

As a rule, _____

Ⅳ Finishing Touches for Chapter 9

次のテーマで一つのパラグラフを英文で書きましょう。

テーマ：スポーツにまつわる私のエピソード

条　件：パラグラフライティングの手法を用いて書く。2つ以上の「一般化」するつなぎ言葉を用いる。単語数は 100 words 程度とする。

日本には、サッカーや野球、テニスなどをはじめ、あまり知られていないようなものまで、さまざまなスポーツがあります。あなたの好きなスポーツを一つ取り上げて、そのスポーツが好きな理由や魅力など、スポーツにまつわるあなたのエピソードを 1 つのパラグラフにまとめてみましょう。出来上がったら、文書または口頭で発表しましょう。

Paragraph Title: _____

Introduction Sentence: _____

_____

Supporting Sentences: _____

_____

_____

_____

Concluding Sentence: _____

_____

他にもこんな「一般化」するつなぎ言葉があります。

broadly speaking（大まかに言って）**fundamentally**（根本的に）**in most cases**（大抵の場合）**in the main**（おおむね）**most often**（ほとんどの場合）**usually**（通常は）

Brush-up Assignment

「一般化」するつなぎ言葉を使った英文を、辞書や新聞、ネットなどで探して書き出してみましょう。

- _____

- _____

Chapter 10

The Great American Road Trip

車で旅するアメリカ再発見

Aim

Transition Words & Phrases for LOGICAL RELATIONSHIP:

[A] so that（～するために）[A] as a result（その結果）[B] for this reason（このような理由から）

[B] consequently（必然的に）[L] accordingly（従って）[L] in spite of（～にもかかわらず）

Core Idea: travel experiences

WARM-UP

それぞれの語句に合う日本語を選んで、記号を（　）に入れましょう。

1. [A] undertake (　　　)　　　**2.** [A] bet (　　　)　　　**3.** [A] region (　　　)

4. [A] landscape (　　　)　　　**5.** [B] recall (　　　)　　　**6.** [B] thoroughly (　　　)

7. [B] independence (　　　)　　　**8.** [B] prepare for (　　　)　　　**9.** [B] guideline (　　　)

10. [L] attraction (　　　)

a. 景観	b. を実施する	c. 見どころ	d. に備えて準備する	e. 完全に
f. 賭け	g. 指針	h. 地域	i. を思い出させる	j. 独立

READING SECTION

Model Reading A

 38

Traveling across the country is an American tradition that dates back over 100 years. The first cross-country trip in the U.S. by car was undertaken in 1903 by Dr. Horatio Jackson so that he could win a bet. During his 63-day trip, Dr. Jackson met people from all over the country and saw how unique each region of the U.S. was. As a result
5　of his experiences, others were inspired to take the same trip and experience what makes each state special. Today, people continue this tradition and travel across the country to rediscover the U.S. by seeing different landscapes and customs, as well as by meeting new people in each region.

Notes　date back over 以上前にさかのぼる **Dr. Horatio Jackson** ホレイシォ・ジャクソン博士 **(1872-1955)** アメリカ合衆国を自動車で横断した最初の人物 **win a bet** 賭けに勝つ

Ⅰ 本文を読んで、下線部に入るもっとも適切なものを a ～ d より選びましょう。

Dr. Jackson took the U.S.'s first trip across the _____ by automobile in 1903 to win a bet.

　　a. continent　　**b.** border　　**c.** interstate　　**d.** countries

Ⅱ 本文の内容と一致するように、(　　) に適切な一語を書き入れましょう。

Dr. Jackson's trip has inspired others to make the same trip and experience the unique things each (　　　　　) offers.

Ⅲ Model Reading A と同じ内容になるように、次の英文を順に並べ替えましょう。

1. In 1903, Dr. Horatio Jackson took the first cross-country car trip to win a bet.

2. Traveling across the U.S. has been popular for more than 100 years.

3. Other people took the same trip because his experience inspired them.

4. Today, people still travel across the country to see different landscapes and traditions and to meet new people.

5. During his trip, he met people from all over the country and discovered each region was unique.

　　　　　(　　) → (　　) → (　　) → (　　) → (　　)

Model Reading B 39

Road trips refer to traveling with family or friends by car to "far away" places they would not usually visit. Road trips recall a time before the country was thoroughly explored and inspire the sense of adventure and independence that Americans highly value. For this reason, today, the road trip is an annual tradition for many families. When preparing for a road trip, families follow the same guidelines that Dr. Jackson did, and consequently, they pack food and may even bring pets along for longer trips. A road trip is a special occasion when families travel together and head for a family adventure in a new place.

I 本文を読んで、下線部に入るもっとも適切なものを a 〜 d より選びましょう。

When _____ for a road trip, families pack food and may even bring pets for longer trips.

    a. returning   **b.** going   **c.** considering   **d.** preparing

II 本文の内容と一致するように、（　　）に適切な一語を書き入れましょう。

Road trips remind people of a time (　　　　　　) the country was thoroughly explored.

III Model Reading B と同じ内容になるように、次の英文の下線部に適切な語句を書き入れましょう。

Main Idea: Road trips mean _____ by car to _____ places with family or friends.

Supporting Details:

1. They are reminders of a time when the country was not fully _____ and represent _____ and _____.

2. Road trips are now a yearly _____ for many families.

3. Families follow Dr. Jackson's _____ and bring _____ and _____ for longer trips.

Conclusion: Road trips are a _____ time for families to travel together and have a fun _____ in a new place.

Ⅳ Reading A と Reading B にそれぞれ適したタイトルを英語で書きましょう。

Reading A : _____

Reading B : _____

Ⅰ 次の会話文を聞いて空欄を埋めましょう。

A: I've heard that road trips are popular in America (¹ _____) to the large size of the country.

B: That's true! In spite of being the same country, there are 50 states, and each state is unique.

A: What kinds of things do people (² _____) on road trips?

B: Regional foods and (³ _____) are quite popular. There are also roadside attractions along every highway in the U.S.

A: What sort of things are roadside attractions?

B: A roadside attraction can be (⁴ _____). Kansas, for example, has the World's Largest Ball of Twine. Each state has its own (⁵ _____) of attraction.

A: With so much to do, many people plan more than one trip.

B: That's right. It's a big country, and accordingly, many people plan a road trip every year to see (⁶ _____) things.

Notes **World's Largest Ball of Twine** 世界最大の麻ひも玉 **with so much to do** やりたいことがたくさんあるために

Ⅱ 質問を聞いて、正しい答えを a ～ c から選びましょう。

1. a   b   c

2. a   b   c

WRITING SECTION

✔ **「論理的関係」に関するつなぎ言葉をうまく使うためのヒント**
論理的関係でのつなぎ言葉の役割は、前後の文のつながりをわかりやすく示し、論旨が論理的につながっていくように表現することです。そのためには、文章の流れがどちらに向かうべきかを明確に示す言葉を使うことが必要です。原因→結果、理由→帰結の関係がはっきりとわかるように文章を書きましょう。

本文で取り上げた以外に、次のような「論理的関係」を示すつなぎ言葉があります。
but then again（しかしまた一方）**even though**（〜なのに）**hence**（このような訳で）
however（しかしながら）**in consequence**（その結果）**notwithstanding**（[前置詞] 〜にもかかわらず）**with that in mind**（その点 [こと] を念頭に入れて）**yet**（けれども）

「論理的関係」を示すつなぎ言葉の具体的な使い方をみてみましょう。
■ 前の事から類推される結果や結論が続く。
1. Transportation costs are a major expense for the industry. **Hence**, the location of factories is an important concern.
   （産業界にとって、交通費は大きな出費である。**したがって**、工場の立地は重要な関心事である）

2. **In consequence**, I decided to use a simple statistical method to characterize the data.
   （**その結果**、私は簡単な統計的手法でデータを特徴づけることにした）

3. **With that in mind**, we should start the project earlier.
   （**そう考えると**、もっと早くからプロジェクトをスタートさせるべきですね）

■ 前の事柄や理由に反する結果や結論が続く。
4. This hypothesis may be correct. **But then again**, it may be completely wrong.
   （この仮説は正しいかもしれない。**しかしまた**、完全に間違っている可能性もある）

5. **Notwithstanding** his inexperience, he got the job easily.
   （未経験**にもかかわらず**、彼は難なくその仕事を手に入れた）

6. It may be unexpected news. **Yet**, it is true.
   （思いもよらないニュースかもしれない。**だが**、それは真実である）

日本語の文法では、順接（の接続詞）、逆接（の接続詞）として学びますが、英語の文法では特にこのような分類として教えていません。resultative construction（結果構文）やcontradictory conjunction（逆接）もあまり馴染みがない表現かもしれません。しかし、英語の場合は、前置詞、接続詞、副詞、接続詞の役目をする副詞など、品詞が順接、逆接の役目を果たします。したがって、前置詞の後には名詞、that（接続詞）の後には節がくるといった約束事をきちんと守って文を書く必要があります。そのためには、品詞を理解したりイディオムをしっかりと身につけることが必要になってくるのです。

Ⅰ 次のそれぞれの英文にもっとも適したつなぎ言葉を下の選択肢から選びましょう。文頭に来る語は大文字で書き始めましょう。

1. I had to cancel my plans (   ) my sudden illness.

2. I know we are short on time, but (   ), let's finish the most important tasks first.

3. The weather forecast said it would rain today. (   ), it has been sunny all morning.

4. I failed to turn in my assignment on time, (   ) I will receive a lower grade.

even if,   hence,   because of,   however,   as a result,   with that in mind

Ⅱ 与えられた語句を使って、次の日本語を英語にしましょう。

1. 日本にいるのに、うちの会社では英語が公用語になっています。
(even though, official language)

_____

2. 私のペーパーは冗長だと指摘された。それを受けて、私は文章を短くした。
(redundant, accordingly)

_____

3. 天候不順にもかかわらず、野菜の価格は比較的安定している。(notwithstanding, stable)

_____

Ⅲ Let's practice transitions!

例文にならって、文を作ってみましょう。

例文

1. The first cross-country trip in the U.S. by car was undertaken in 1903 by Dr. Horatio Jackson **so that** he could win a bet.

(**Your original**)

_____ **so that**

_____

2. (a) Americans greatly value adventure and independence.

(b) **For this reason**, the road trip is an annual tradition for many families.

(**Your original**)

(a) _____

(b) **For this reason**, _____

3. **In spite of** being the same country, there are 50 states, and each state is unique.

(**Your original**)

In spite of _____

次のテーマで一つのパラグラフを英文で書きましょう。

> **テーマ**：旅に関する話題
>
> **条　件**：パラグラフライティングの手法を用いて書く。２つ以上の「論理的関係」を
> 表すつなぎ言葉を用いる。単語数は 100 words 程度とする。

本文では、さまざまな風景や伝統を見たり新しい人と出会うために、旅に出ることが述べられていますが、あなたには、どんな思い出の旅行があるでしょうか。これまでに経験した旅行にまつわる思い出、旅先での貴重な体験、グルメ、あるいはまた世界で一番行ってみたい場所のことなど、旅に関する話題をテーマにして、1 つのパラグラフを書いてみましょう。出来上がったら、文書または口頭で発表しましょう。

Paragraph Title: _____

Introduction Sentence: _____

_____

Supporting Sentences: _____

_____

_____

_____

Concluding Sentence: _____

_____

他にもこんな「論理的関係」を表すつなぎ言葉があります。

because（〜なので）**based on that**（それを踏まえて）**even if**（仮に〜だとしても）**nevertheless / none the less**（それでもやはり）**since**（〜なので）**therefore**（その結果として）**thus**（こういう訳で）

Brush-up Assignment

「論理的関係」を表すつなぎ言葉を使った英文を、辞書や新聞、ネットなどで探して書き出してみましょう。

- _____

_____

- _____

_____

Chapter 11 *Writing a Strong Main Character*

ソーシャルメディアに投稿する

Aim

Transition Words & Phrases for PREPARATION

^A plan for (〜の計画を立てる) ^A indicate ([方向性を] 指し示す) ^B plan to (〜する方針を立てる)

Core Idea: ways to express ourselves on social media

○ WARM-UP ○

それぞれの語句に合う日本語を選んで、記号を（ ）に入れましょう。

1. ^A verbal ( )　　　2. ^A oral story ( )　　　3. ^A literate ( )

4. ^A billion ( )　　　5. ^B require ( )　　　6. ^B poster ( )

7. ^B primary ( )　　　8. ^B immerse ( )　　　9. ^L to begin with ( )

10. ^L platform ( )

---

a. 口で語られる物語　　　b. 言葉による　　　c.（利用者と提供者をつなぐ）場

d. 投稿者　　　e. を必要とする　　　f. 読み書きができる　　　g.（人を）熱中させる

h. まず第一に　　　i. 10 億　　　j. 主要な

READING SECTION

Model Reading A

 42

      Humans have passed stories down in verbal and written form for thousands of years. Stories help people plan for the future by understanding the past and present. Historically, most people have been unable to read, which meant they could only enjoy oral stories. In the 21st century, most people are literate and have access to social media as a means

5 to read and tell stories. More than four billion people use the internet every day, and the traffic on social media sites indicates that most internet users love telling, hearing, and reading stories.

Notes   **pass down** を伝える **have access to** を利用できる **traffic** アクセス数

Ⅰ 本文を読んで、下線部に入るもっとも適切なものを a 〜 d より選びましょう。

Before global literacy rates improved, most people could not read and could only enjoy _____ stories.

    a. short   **b.** easy   **c.** oral   **d.** picture

Ⅱ 本文の内容と一致するように、（　　　）に適切な一語を書き入れましょう。

Today, most people are (　　　　　　) and can read and tell stories through social media posts.

Ⅲ Model Reading A と同じ内容になるように、次の英文を順に並べ替えましょう。

1. With over four billion social media users daily, most internet users enjoy reading and telling stories.

2. Most people are literate in the 21st century, and with access to social media, they are able to read and tell stories.

3. For thousands of years humans have been telling stories in verbal and written forms.

4. These stories help us understand the past and present, so we can plan for the future.

5. Before, many people could not read, so they shared oral stories.

        (　　　) → (　　　) → (　　　) → (　　　) → (　　　)

Model Reading B

 43

One of the posting features on Instagram, a social media site with over one billion users, is called "Stories." This naming suggests "telling a story" to communicate your ideas on the site. A story requires a character and an event. On Instagram, for example, the poster is the primary character, and posts often show movements of personal growth or change. When posting a story, plan to share photos and videos because images help immerse the reader in the story. Everyone loves a good story, and using Instagram and other social media is a great way to share personal stories and make friends.

Notes ┈┈┈
posting features 投稿機能 **images** 画像

Ⅰ 本文を読んで、下線部に入るもっとも適切なものを a 〜 d より選びましょう。

In social media stories, the poster is the _____, and the story they share often shows growth and change.

    a. main character　　**b.** creator　　**c.** editor　　**d.** plot

Ⅱ 本文の内容と一致するように、（　）に適切な一語を書き入れましょう。

Images are useful in getting the reader engaged in the (　　　　　).

Ⅲ Model Reading B と同じ内容になるように、次の英文の下線部に適切な語句を書き入れましょう。

Main Idea: One of the posting features of Instagram, with over _____ users, is called _____.

Supporting Details:

1. Stories require _____ and events.

2. For example, the _____ is the primary character on Instagram, and post often include scenes of personal _____ and _____.

3. When posting stories, _____ to share photos and videos.

4. _____ are a great way to draw readers into the story.

Conclusion: Using social media such as Instagram is an excellent way to share _____ stories and make _____.

IV Reading A と Reading B にそれぞれ適したタイトルを英語で書きましょう。

Reading A : _____

Reading B : _____

LISTENING SECTION

CD 44、45

I 次の会話文を聞いて空欄を埋めましょう。

A: I know social media is not for everyone, but I really like it. I (^{1})
enjoy reading posts from other countries.

B: I agree. To begin with, social media allows people to (^{2}) with other
places and ideas.

A: It does! Seeing pictures and posts from other people's lives can teach us more
about the world.

B: That is true. Social media has created a (^{3}) with the aim of
creating a global community.

A: Do you know my favorite part? I can have friends all over the world!

(^{4}) to social media, I did not know anyone from a different country.

B: I like that too; I enjoy (^{5}) from people who live in other countries.

A: What do you think is the best part of social media?

B: Most importantly, rarely told stories from (^{6}) groups can be heard
and read by everyone.

II 質問を聞いて、正しい答えを a ～ c から選びましょう。

1. a   b   c

2. a   b   c

WRITING SECTION

> ✔ 「準備」を表すつなぎ言葉をうまく使うためのヒント
>
> 「準備」を表すつなぎ言葉は、行事や作業を行う際の「最初の」行動や、「事前に」やっておくべき事柄などを提示するときに使います。「〜に備えて」「〜の準備として」など、準備する目的や方法、過程を説明するときにも、決まった表現として覚えておくと「準備」に関する話題をスムーズに伝えることができます。

本文で取り上げた以外に、次のような「準備」を表すつなぎ言葉があります。

at the outset of（〜の冒頭で）**in anticipation of**（〜を見込んで）**in preparation for**（〜に向けて）**prior to**（〜に先立って）**the initial stage**（最初の段階）**with a view to**（〜を視野に入れて）

「準備」を表すつなぎ言葉の具体的な使い方をみてみましょう。

■「最初」であることを伝える

1. **Initially**, I was reluctant to share this personal story on X, but I think it is an important topic, so here goes!

   （**当初**、この個人的な話を X でシェアすることに抵抗がありましたが、重要なテーマだと思うので、ここで公開することにしました！）

2. **First of all**, I will provide followers with some background before going into details.

   （**まずは**、詳細を述べる前に、フォロワーに背景を説明します）

3. **The first step** in creating a successful TikTok video is to identify your target audience and tailor your content to their interests.

   （成功する TikTok 動画を作成する**最初のステップ**は、ターゲットオーディエンスを特定し、彼らの興味に合わせたコンテンツを作成することだ）

■「事前」であることを伝える

4. **Before** posting my story on Facebook, I will edit it carefully to ensure it is error-free.

   （Facebook に投稿する**前に**、誤字脱字がないように丁寧に編集します）

5. We need to discuss our plans **beforehand** to avoid any confusion.

   （混乱を避けるために、**事前に**話し合う必要がある）

6. Be sure to prepare your presentation materials well **in advance**.

   （プレゼン資料は**事前に**しっかり準備しておきましょう）

For Your Information and Guidance

ネットで使える表現

Click/Hit/Smash the like button.（いいねボタンを押してくださいね）

Click the Like and Subscribe button!（いいねと登録ボタンをクリックしてください）

Press/Click the like button and leave a comment below.

（いいねボタンとコメントをお願いします）

subscribe（チャンネル登録）video（動画）like（いいねする）

Instagram-worthy, Insta-worthy, Instagenic, Instagrammable（インスタ映えする）

I 次のそれぞれの英文にもっとも適したつなぎ言葉を下の選択肢から選びましょう。文頭に来る語は大文字で書き始めましょう。

1. (   ), I want to thank all my followers for their support.

2. (   ) to releasing the website, I thoroughly reexamined the format.

3. I will research some related topics (   ) for my upcoming blog post.

4. I hesitated to share my story at the (   ), but now I'm glad I did.

> in preparation, before, prior, with a view to, initial stage, first of all

---

II 与えられた語句を使って、次の日本語を英語にしましょう。

1. 授業の冒頭で、教授は今日の講義で使われる主要な語彙の定義をした。
(at the outset of, key vocabulary words)

_____

2. このサイトを訪れる多くの人を想定して、さまざまな角度からの意見を掲載することにした。(in anticipation of, post)

_____

3. インスタ映えする写真を撮るために、その場所の日没前の時間を事前に確認した。
(Insta-worthy image, in advance)

_____

Ⅲ Let's practice transitions!

例文にならって、文を作ってみましょう。

例文

1. Stories help people **plan for** the future by understanding the past and present.

Your original

_____ **plan for** _____

_____

2. The traffic on social media sites seems to **indicate** that most internet users love telling, hearing, and reading stories.

Your original

_____ **indicate** _____

_____

3. When posting a story, **plan to** share photos and videos.

Your original

_____ **plan to** _____

_____

次のテーマの中からトピックを一つ選び、一つのパラグラフを英文で書きましょう。

> **テーマ**：- Instagram や SNS の投稿で私のお気に入りのもの
> - 私はこんなふうにソーシャルメディアで自分を表現しています
> - 「いいね」（LIKE）をたくさんもらった私のブログ（X、画像など）を紹介します
> -SNS で発信するときに気をつけたいこと
>
> **条　件**：パラグラフライティングの手法を用いて書く。2つ以上の「準備」を表すつなぎ言葉を用いる。単語数は 100 words 程度とする。

あなたのホームページや X、インスタグラムなどのソーシャルメディアで、あなたが自分をどのように表現しているか紹介してください。ソーシャルメディアを使っていない人は、SNS で発信する場合の注意点を1つのパラグラフにまとめてみましょう。出来上がったら、文書または口頭で発表しましょう。

Paragraph Title: _____

Introduction Sentence: _____

_____

Supporting Sentences: _____

_____

_____

Concluding Sentence: _____

_____

他にもこんな「準備」を表すつなぎ言葉があります。

ahead of time（前もって）**as a first step**（第一歩として）**at first**（初めは）**at the beginning of**（〜の初めに）**first**（最初に）**get ready for**（〜の準備をする）**in advance of**（〜より前［先］に）**in the beginning**（最初は）**preceding**（[名詞の前のみで] 前の）**to start off**（まず手始めに）

Brush-up Assignment

「準備」を表すつなぎ言葉を使った英文を、辞書や新聞、ネットなどで探して書き出してみましょう。

- _____
- _____

Chapter 12

Effective Email Writing Standards

効果的なメールを書く

Aim

Transition Words & Phrases for DETAILS:

[A] specifically（具体的には）[B] especially（とりわけ）[B] including（［前置詞］〜を含めて）

[L] in particular（特に）

Core Idea: learning to write effective emails

WARM-UP

それぞれの語句に合う日本語を選んで、記号を（　）に入れましょう。

1. [A] preferred (　　　)　　**2.** [A] alternative (　　　)　　**3.** [A] conventional (　　　)

4. [A] brief (　　　)　　**5.** [A] structure (　　　)　　**6.** [B] acquire (　　　)

7. [B] crucial (　　　)　　**8.** [B] identify (　　　)　　**9.** [B] respond (　　　)

10. [L] leave out (　　　)

a. 従来型の	b. 望ましい	c. 極めて重要な	d. を省く	e. 確認する
f. 返答する	g. 構成	h. を習得する	i. 簡潔な	j. 代替手段

Model Reading A 46

Electronic mail, or email, has become the preferred alternative to letters in modern business and educational environments. The rules for writing emails differ from those for writing conventional letters. Specifically, the structure of an email is entirely different from that of a letter. Emails favor brief, action-oriented messages over lengthy
5 ones. Structurally, the subject line of an email introduces the topic, the first paragraph introduces the direction of the email, and the final section concludes the message and invites a response. Concise and easy-to-understand emails are desirable for efficient communication. In summary, email has become the preferred mode of communication, and knowing the unique rules for writing emails is important.

Notes ....
action-oriented 行動を重視した **lengthy** 長々とした **structurally** 構造的には **subject line** 件名

Ⅰ 本文を読んで、下線部に入るもっとも適切なものを a 〜 d より選びましょう。

Email has replaced the _____ as the preferred form of business communication.
   a. text   **b.** message   **c.** telegram   **d.** letter

Ⅱ 本文の内容と一致するように、（　　）に適切な一語を書き入れましょう。

Brief, active statements are preferred over (　　　　　　　), passive sentences when composing email messages.

Ⅲ Model Reading A と同じ内容になるように英文を順に並べ替えましょう。

1. For efficient communication, short and clear emails are desirable.

2. In modern business and educational situations, email has become the preferred alternative to letters.

3. The structure of an email is fixed: the subject line introduces the topic, the first paragraph sets the direction of the email, and the last section completes the message and asks for a reply.

4. Because email is such a prevalent means of communication, it is necessary to understand how to write effective emails.

5. However, the methods for writing emails differ from those for writing conventional letters.

(　　) → (　　) → (　　) → (　　) → (　　)

Model Reading B

 47

　Acquiring the basics of writing emails is crucial, especially given their instant delivery. Many short emails can be sent to communicate effectively instead of one long letter or memo. Therefore, concision is vital in email writing, with a clear structure so that a reader can quickly identify the topic, the important information, and the expected action, including how and when to respond. In addition, summarizing the purpose of the email and reiterating the request in a reader-friendly tone is desirable. It is also essential to leave room for questions to facilitate discussion. Mastering these tips will make email writing less strenuous, leading to successful communication.

Notes　**given**［前置詞］〜を考慮すると **concision** 簡潔さ **reiterating the request** 依頼内容を再度伝えること **in a reader-friendly tone** 読む人にわかりやすい表現で **leave room for** の余地を残す **strenuous** 非常に骨の折れる

Ⅰ 本文を読んで、下線部に入るもっとも適切なものを a 〜 d より選びましょう。

When you conclude the email, consider giving the reader room for discussion or posing _____.

　a. a subject　　**b.** a challenge　　**c.** topics　　**d.** questions

Ⅱ 本文の内容と一致するように、（　　）に適切な一語を書き入れましょう。

If the points are specific, readers will quickly determine how to (　　　　　　　　).

Ⅲ Model Reading B と同じ内容になるように、次の英文の下線部に適切な語句を書き入れましょう。

Main Idea: It is very important to learn the _____ of writing emails.

Supporting Details:

1. Instead of one long letter or memo, people can send many _____ quickly.

2. The main principle for writing an email is to be _____.

3. Emails should have a clear _____, so the reader can easily understand the _____, important _____, and expected _____.

4. Summarize the _____ of the email, restate any _____ in a friendly way, and invite the reader to ask questions or continue the _____.

Conclusion: Learning these _____ will make email writing easier and _____ more successful communication.

Ⅳ Reading A と Reading B にそれぞれ適したタイトルを英語で書きましょう。

Reading A : _____

Reading B : _____

LISTENING SECTION

CD 48、49

Ⅰ 次の会話文を聞いて空欄を埋めましょう。

A: Do you have any tips for writing business emails? I want to make a good
(^{1}) on my bosses.

B: Of course! The most important thing is to identify the (^{2}) of the
email quickly and clearly.

A: Should I get right to the point and leave out introductions?

B: Well, yes and no. I (^{3}) including a friendly greeting at the beginning
in particular, and getting to the point right afterward.

A: Then I should explain all the details fully, right?

B: Not (^{4}). Many people receive hundreds of emails per day, so it's
best to keep them short.

A: Short emails are better, because people are so busy, and that makes
(^{5}). From now on, I can improve my work emails, especially by
being clear and to the point.

B: Remember to be friendly, and always ask for help if (^{6})!

Notes ....
get right to the point 直接要点に触れる **right afterwards** その後で **from now on** 今後は **to the
point** 要領よく

Ⅱ 質問を聞いて、正しい答えを a ～ c から選びましょう。

1. a   b   c

2. a   b   c

WRITING SECTION ⟩

✔ 状況を「詳細」に述べるつなぎ言葉をうまく使うためのヒント

状況を「詳細」に述べるつなぎ言葉は、議論や論点を裏付けるための詳しい説明や事例を提供するために用います。具体的な例をあげたり、論点を明確にしたり、主張を裏付ける根拠を示したりする際に便利です。「詳細」に述べるつなぎ言葉を使うと、読む人はあなたが説明している内容を明確に把握し、焦点化できるようになります。

本文で取り上げた以外に、次のような「詳細」に述べるつなぎ言葉があります。
above all else（何にもまして）**in fact**（実は、実のところ）**in other words**（言い換えれば）
in particular（特に）**in regard to**（に関しては）**to be specific**（具体的に言うと）

「詳細」に述べるつなぎ言葉の具体的な使い方をみてみましょう。

1. **Actually**, the meaning of this paragraph is unclear.
   （**実際のところ**、このパラグラフは意味がはっきりしない）

2. **Furthermore**, the conclusion is too abstract.
   （さらに、結論は抽象的過ぎる）

3. I will now explain these issues **in detail**.
   （これらの問題点について、これから**詳しく**説明します）

4. **Particularly**, the first sentence is quite misleading.
   （**とりわけ**、最初の文章は誤解を招きそうだ）

5. I had a cake **specially** made for your birthday.
   （きみの誕生日のために**特別に**ケーキを作ってもらったんだ）

6. Young people **especially** like this kind of music.
   （若者は**特に**この種の音楽を好む）

7. Drive quietly, **especially when** schools are nearby.
   （**特に**学校が近くにあるときは、静かに運転しましょう）

   注意して使いましょう：particularly、specially、especially は同じ意味で使うこともありますが、どれを使うか迷ったときは、particularly は特定の場面や事柄に焦点を当てて「とりわけ」、specially は特定の目的や機会のために行われた（作られた）ものを指して「特別に」、especially は同じグループや特定の状況のなかのものと比べて「特に」、というニュアンスの違いで使い分けましょう。

I 次のそれぞれの英文にもっとも適したつなぎ言葉を下の選択肢から選びましょう。文頭に来る語は大文字で書き始めましょう。

1. (   ) your inquiry, the project will be completed by the end of the year.

2. When designing a new building, safety must be a top priority (   ).

3. These dishes are very tasty. (   ), the restaurant has won numerous awards for its excellent cuisine.

4. Running in the morning keeps my body awake and energized. (   ), it helps me stay in shape.

> in detail,   above all else,   in fact,   to demonstrate,   furthermore,
>
> in regard to

II 与えられた語句を使って、次の日本語を英語にしましょう。

1. 世の中にはさまざまな情報があふれているが、特にインターネットは、子どもたちに新しい情報を与えている。(flooding, in particular)

_____

2. 新しいソフトの更新により、システムの性能が向上します。つまり、より速く、より効率的になります。(system's performance, in other words)

_____

3. 私たちはマーケティング戦略を改善する必要がある。具体的には、メールキャンペーンに力を入れるべきだ。(marketing strategy, to be specific, email campaigns)

_____

Ⅲ Let's practice transitions!

例文にならって、文を作ってみましょう。

例文

1. (a) The rules for writing emails differ from those for writing conventional letters.

   (b) **Specifically**, the structure of an email is entirely different from that of an essay.

Your original

   (a) _____

   (b) **Specifically**, _____

2. Acquiring the basics of writing emails is crucial, **especially** given their instant delivery.

Your original

   _____

   especially _____

3. A reader can quickly identify the topic, the important information, and the expected action, **including** how and when to respond.

Your original

   _____

   including _____

Ⅳ Finishing Touches for Chapter 12

次のテーマで一通のメールを英文で書きましょう。

> **テーマ**：先生に依頼のメールを書く
>
> **条　件**：以下の書式を使って書く。2つ以上の「詳細」のつなぎ言葉を用いる。単語
> 数は 100 words 程度とする。

プロジェクト（あるいは別の事柄）に関するサポートを依頼するメールを、先生に書きましょう。メールには、件名、相手の名前、少なくとも2つの「詳細」のつなぎ言葉、あなたの名前を入れてください。出来上がったメールは、文書または口頭で発表しましょう。

Subject line: _____

The opening greeting: _____

The main points: _____

The detail: _____

_____

_____

_____

Conclusion with a closing greeting: _____

_____

Your name: _____

他にもこんな「詳細」に述べるつなぎ言葉があります。

above all（何よりもまず、とりわけ）**additionally**（加えて）**among others**（数ある中でも、何よりも）**besides**（その上、更にまた）**in addition**（その上）**moreover**（その上に）**notably**（特に、とりわけ）**such as**（例えば〜など）

Brush-up Assignment

「詳細」に述べるつなぎ言葉を使った英文を、辞書や新聞、ネットなどで探して書き出してみましょう。

- _____

_____

- _____

_____

Skills for Job-Hunting

就活に必要なスキルを身につける

Aim

Transition Words & Phrases or RESTATEMENT

[A] basically（基本的に見て） [A] to put it differently（言い換えれば） [B] in essence（本質的には）

[L] put differently（別の表現で言うと）

Core Idea: communication skills in a professional setting

WARM-UP

それぞれの語句に合う日本語を選んで、記号を（　）に入れましょう。

1. [A] value（　　）　**2.** [A] highlight（　　）　**3.** [A] resumé（　　）　**4.** [A] qualification（　　）

5. [A] career（　　）　**6.** [B] targeted（　　）　**7.** [B] ensure（　　）　**8.** [B] diligence（　　）

9. [B] respect（　　）　**10.** [L] what if（　　）

a. 履歴書　b. 勤勉　c. 〜してしまったらどうしよう　d. を評価する　e. を確実にする
f. 的を絞った　　g. を強調する　　h. 経歴　　i. 敬意を払うこと　　j. 資格

Model Reading A

 50

Understanding appropriate communication standards is crucial for success in professional settings. Basically, employers value employees with strong communication skills, so highlighting these skills in your resumé is essential. This document briefly summarizes your education, experience, and qualifications, making it the most crucial
5 tool in your career. An English resumé should be kept concise at one or two pages, as reviewers must read through every application. Therefore, shorter resumés are preferred, as they are easier to read and more likely to receive a job offer. To put it differently, creating a concise and impactful resumé with a focus on communication skills is a strategy that will get you a job offer and help you succeed professionally.

Notes   **professional setting** 仕事の場、職場   **reviewer** 書類選考担当者

Ⅰ 本文を読んで、下線部に入るもっとも適切なものを a 〜 d より選びましょう。

A professional English _____ should be 1-2 pages long.
    a. letter   **b.** email   **c.** resumé   **d.** interview

Ⅱ 本文の内容と一致するように、( ) に適切な一語を書きましょう。

A short resumé is easier to read and more (   ) to lead to a job offer.

Ⅲ Model Reading A と同じ内容になるように、次の英文を順に並べ替えましょう。

1. Like many professional documents in English, it should be brief, usually only one or two pages.

2. Good communication skills are necessary for professional success.

3. Thus, creating a clear, impressive resumé highlighting communication skills help you get a job offer and succeed in your career.

4. Your resumé is critical for your career because it summarizes your education, experience, and qualifications.

5. Employers appreciate workers possessing good communication abilities, so it is vital to emphasize these skills in your resumé.

            (   ) → (   ) → (   ) → (   ) → (   )

Model Reading B

 51

  After creating an impressive resumé, the next critical step is to apply for the position you want and get an interview. There are two ways to conduct an interview: verbally or by answering written questions. In the latter case, it is essential to answer questions in a concise and targeted manner and to ensure that you have answers to all questions. During
5 the verbal interview, maintain eye contact with the interviewer, use polite language, and demonstrate your reliability and diligence. Politeness and showing respect are crucial traits that many interviewers appreciate and value. In essence, being courteous and professional throughout the interview process is imperative after preparing an outstanding resumé.

Notes ....
verbally 口頭で **reliability** 信頼度 **trait** 特性 **imperative** 必要不可欠の

I 本文を読んで、下線部に入るもっとも適切なものを a～d から選びましょう。

In the case of a _____ interview, it is essential that you answer all given questions.
  a. written   **b.** verbal   **c.** face-to-face   **d.** spoken

II 本文の内容と一致するように、（　　）に適切なものを書きましょう。

Many (　　　　　　) appreciate it when you use courteous expressions and behave respectfully during the interview.

III Model Reading B と同じ内容になるように、次の英文の下線部に適切な語句を書きましょう。

Main Idea: After preparing a good resumé, the next step is _____ and _____ for a job.

Supporting Details:

1. Interviews can be done by _____ or by answering _____.
2. If you answer in writing, keep your responses _____ , _____ , and make sure you answer _____.
3. During the interview, look at the _____, and use _____.
4. This will show that you are _____.
5. Most interviewers will have a good _____ of you if you are respectful and polite.

Conclusion: So, after you _____ a good resumé, remember to be polite and professional during the _____.

IV Reading A と Reading B にそれぞれ適したタイトルを英語で書きましょう。

Reading A : _____

Reading B : _____

LISTENING SECTION

CD 52、53

I 次の会話文を聞いて空欄を埋めましょう。

A: I hate work communications! They are so (¹   ), and I never know what to say.

B: I'm sorry to hear that! Is there something in (²   ) that's stressing you out?

A: I feel like I say too much or too little in my emails, and I worry I'm not polite enough.

B: Remember to say your position clearly and concisely when communicating at work to (³   ) misunderstandings.

A: What if I forget something important?

B: That's OK; people always forget things, and it's rarely a problem. Put differently, (⁴   ) that your co-workers will ask you if they don't understand something.

A: I see! How polite should I be with work colleagues, in (⁵   )?

B: That's a tough question to answer. You should be polite but not overly (⁶   ) with colleagues.

Notes ....
work communications 職場でのコミュニケーション **stress you out** あなたをストレスで疲れさせる **co-worker** 同僚

II 質問を聞いて、正しい答えを a ~ c から選びましょう。

1. a   b   c

2. a   b   c

> ## WRITING SECTION

✔ 「言い直し」のつなぎ言葉をうまく使うためのヒント

「言い直し」のつなぎ言葉は、複雑なアイデアを要約したり、明確な説明をしたり、読者が完全に理解できるようにポイントを再確認したりするのに便利です。レポートなどで、同じ言葉を繰り返して使うと、文章が単調になってしまいます。同じ内容を伝えるときでも、重複した語を使用することは避けて、別の語に置き換えましょう。

本文で取り上げた以外に、次のような「言い直し」のつなぎ言葉があります。

as discussed above（前述の通り）**as discussed previously**（前に述べたように）**as I have already said**（前にも言ったように）**as noted above**（上に指摘したように）**briefly speaking**（簡単に言うと）**in brief**（要するに）**in short**（手短に言えば）**namely**（すなわち）**that is**（つまり）**to put it another way**（別の言い方をすれば）

「言い直し」のつなぎ言葉の具体的な使い方をみてみましょう。

1. **Briefly speaking**, the structure of this sentence has a double meaning.
   （**簡単に言うと**、この文の構造には二重の意味がある）

   〜ly（副詞）+ speaking は「〜的に言えば」という慣用句です。
   briefly/generally/strictly/technically speaking（[簡潔に、一般的に、厳密に、専門的に] 言えば）speaking を省略しても同じ意味で使えます。

2. The most difficult part of writing a paragraph is the first sentence. **To put it another way**, the first sentence is the most challenging.
   （パラグラフを書くのに一番難しいのは、最初の文です。**別の言い方をすれば**、文の冒頭が最も難しいです）

   to put it another way（別の言い方をすれば）は、本文で使われている **to put it differently** と同じように、自分が何か発言した後に、異なる言い方で言い直したいときに使います。この場合の put は to express in words（言葉で表現する）という意味です。

3. **As discussed above**, the majority of people agree with his conclusions.
   （**前述のように**、大多数の人は彼の結論に同意している）

   as discussed above（前述の通り）**as noted above**（上に指摘したように）**as discussed previously**（前に述べたように）は、文章中で「前の部分に書いてあること」についてまた触れるといった時に、「as（接続詞）+過去分詞+ above（副詞）」の形で使います。

冒頭で取り上げた最初の言い直しのつなぎ言葉は briefly（brief［形容詞］ + -ly）speaking で、「簡潔に言えば」という意味でした。では、in brief や in short は、後ろに名詞がないのに「前置詞＋形容詞」の形であることに違和感を覚えた人はいませんか？　実はこの brief と short は形容詞（簡潔な、簡潔な）ではなく、「簡潔な文」「要約」という意味の名詞なのです。つまり、in conclusion（要するに）in summary（要点としては）in other words（言い換えれば）と同じ「前置詞＋名詞」の形だと理解すれば、スッキリしますね。

Ⅰ 次のそれぞれの英文にもっとも適したつなぎ言葉を下の選択肢から選びましょう。文頭に来る語は大文字で書き始めましょう。

1. The story was long and complicated, but (　　　　　　　　　), very interesting.

2. Strictly (　　　　　　　), what you are doing is not prohibited by the rules.

3. The fall semester began last week, (　　　　　　　　), the first week of September.

4. (　　　　　　　　), the project deadline is next Friday, so make sure to meet the due date.

> speaking,　　as noted above,　　namely,　　essentially,　　other words,
> in short

Ⅱ 与えられた語句を使って、次の日本語を英語にしましょう。

1. 簡単に言えば、私のペーパーの要点は次の３点に要約されます。(briefly speaking)

   _____

2. レポートでは最低でも C を取りたい。つまり、この科目は絶対に落とせない。
   (that is, this subject)

   _____

3. 彼のプレゼンは分かりにくかった。別の言い方をすれば、要点が明確でなかった。
   (to put it another way)

   _____

Ⅲ Let's practice transitions!

例文にならって、文を作ってみましょう。

[例文]

1. (a) Understanding appropriate communication standards is crucial for success in professional settings.

    (b) **Basically**, employers value employees with strong communication skills, making it essential to highlight these skills in your resumé.

[Your original]

(a) _____

(b) **Basically**, _____

2. (a) Shorter resumés are preferred, as they are easier to read and more likely to receive a job offer.

    (b) **To put it differently**, creating a concise and impactful resumé is a strategy that will get you a job offer and help you succeed professionally.

[Your original]

(a) _____

(b) **To put it differently**, _____

3. (a) Politeness and respect are crucial traits that many interviewers appreciate and value.

    (b) **In essence**, it is imperative to be polite and professional throughout the interview process.

[Your original]

(a) _____

(b) **In essence**, _____

Finishing Touches for Chapter 13

次のテーマで一つのパラグラフを英文で書きましょう。

> **テーマ**：コミュニケーション能力を自己分析する
>
> **条　件**：パラグラフライティングの手法を用いて書く。2つ以上の「言い直し」のつなぎ言葉を用いる。単語数は 100 words 程度とする。

あなたがある職場で働くことを想像してください。その仕事をする上で、どのような専門的なコミュニケーションスキルが必要でしょうか。あなたの得意なコミュニケーションスキルと苦手なコミュニケーションスキルを自己分析し、1つのパラグラフにまとめましょう。出来上がったら、文書または口頭で発表しましょう。

Paragraph Title: _____

Introduction Sentence: _____

_____

Supporting Sentences: _____

_____

_____

_____

Concluding Sentence: _____

_____

他にもこんな「言い直し」のつなぎ言葉があります。

as already noted（すでに言及してきたとおり）**put another way**（言い換えれば）**restate**（あらためて述べる）**stated another way**（言い方を変えれば）**to put it simply**（簡単に言えば）

Brush-up Assignment

「言い直し」のつなぎ言葉を使った英文を、辞書や新聞、ネットなどで探して書き出してみましょう。

- _____

  _____

- _____

  _____

Chapter 14

How to Prepare for a Speech

人前でうまく話すには

Aim

Transition Words & Phrases for SIMILARITY

A correspondingly（これと同じように）B like（［前置詞］～のように）B similarly（同様に）
B analogous to（～に似て）L likewise（同様に）L equally（同じように）

Core Idea: preparing for a speech

WARM-UP

それぞれの語句に合う日本語を選んで、記号を（　）に入れましょう。

1. A audience (　　) **2.** A similar (　　) **3.** A proper (　　) **4.** A confidently (　　)
5. B capture (　　) **6.** B quote (　　) **7.** B statistics (　　) **8.** B boring (　　)
9. B manuscript (　　) **10.** L in advance (　　)

a. 自信をもって　b. 引用　c. 前もって　d. 聴衆　e. 原稿　f. 退屈な
g. 似たような　h. をつかむ　i. 適切な　j. 統計資料

Model Reading A

 54

Few people like public speaking, but everyone will need to give a public speech or interview at some point in their life. Public speeches and interviews can effectively share ideas and job-related information with an audience. Inexperienced public speakers often worry about making mistakes, such as mumbling, forgetting their points, or losing the
5 audience's attention. Correspondingly, many people experience similar problems when giving interviews. Interviews require concise, straightforward answers. Speaking in a low voice, answering questions inadequately, or failing to connect with listeners will damage an interview. Fortunately, proper preparation and rehearsal can reduce speech anxiety and help anyone confidently give speeches and interviews.

Notes **public speaking** 演説、人前で話すこと **inexperienced** 経験不足の **mumbling** （口の中で）もぐもぐ言う話し方 **inadequately** 不適切に

Ⅰ 本文を読んで、下線部に入るもっとも適切なものを a～d より選びましょう。

Fear of public speaking can give a person speech _____.

    a. relief   **b.** discomfort   **c.** anxiety   **d.** practice

Ⅱ 本文の内容と一致するように、（　　）に適切な一語を書きましょう。

One of the reasons interviews don't go well is that the voice is too (　　　　).

Ⅲ Model Reading A と同じ内容になるように、次の英文を順に並べ替えましょう。

1. However, some people worry about making mistakes when speaking in public, while others have similar concerns during interviews.

2. To overcome this, preparing appropriately and practicing beforehand can help reduce anxiety and improve public speaking and interviewing skills.

3. Everyone has to speak publicly or give an interview at some point in their life, even if they don't like it.

4. Consequently, interviews require clear answers and good communication with the audience.

5. Public speeches and interviews are valuable ways to share ideas and job-related information with others.

        (　) → (　) → (　) → (　) → (　)

Model Reading B 55

How do you capture the audience with your speech? Remember that a speech, like a paragraph, contains an introduction, organizing points, and a conclusion. When preparing a speech, many list the order of key talking points. By doing so, the speakers can focus on the topic. Similarly, make a note of quotes or statistics and deliver them precisely during the actual speech. Listening to a speech read is analogous to watching a teacher read from a textbook: boring. Therefore, rehearse the essential points and check the manuscript only when appropriate. Developing your expressive skills in this way, coupled with a well-organized speech structure, ensures your speech will captivate your audience.

Notes ···
make a note of を書き留める **speech read** スピーチの棒読み **coupled with** と相まって **captivate** を魅了する

Ⅰ 本文を読んで、下線部に入るもっとも適切なものを a ～ d より選びましょう。

When preparing your speech, write down the _____ of important talking points so you can focus on your topic.

    a. story   **b.** meaning   **c.** order   **d.** method

Ⅱ 本文の内容と一致するように、（　　）に適切な一語を書きましょう。

(　　) to a paragraph, a speech contains an introduction, organizing matters, and a conclusion.

Ⅲ Model Reading B と同じ内容になるように、次の英文の下線部に適切な語句を書きましょう。

Main Idea: Consider how you can grab your _____ in your speech.

Supporting Details:

1. To do this, you must first determine the _____ of your speech, including the _____, organizing points, and _____.

2. When you begin writing your speech, make outlines of the main _____ you will discuss in your _____.

3. Also, note _____ or _____ carefully to deliver them during the speech.

4. Listening to a _____ can be tedious for the listener, so _____ the necessary parts and refer to the _____ only when necessary.

Conclusion: By organizing your speech as such and rehearsing it, you can _____ that you capture your audience's _____.

Ⅳ Reading A と Reading B にそれぞれ適したタイトルを英語で書きましょう。

Reading A : _____

Reading B : _____

LISTENING SECTION

CD 56、57

Ⅰ 次の会話文を聞いて空欄を埋めましょう。

A: Hey, guess what? I got the job I interviewed for last week!

B: (¹   ), that's excellent! You must be really good at public speaking.

A: Actually, I'm not very good at public speaking. (²   ), I practiced a lot, and it paid off.

B: Did you already know the questions they would ask?

A: No, but I knew what I would need to say, so I practiced them in advance. (³   ), I was prepared to answer their questions!

B: How did you practice?

A: I recorded myself answering questions I thought they would ask. Then I watched the video and (⁴   ) when I made a mistake, like stumbling or not speaking clearly.

B: I see! You spent time practicing so you'd feel comfortable. (⁵   ), you took notes when you made mistakes so you'd be fully prepared. That's very smart!

A: Thank you! This kind of practice can help anyone, and it can be (⁶   ) fun watching yourself on video!

Notes **pay off** 報われる **stumbling** 言葉に詰まること

Ⅱ 質問を聞いて、正しい答えを a ～ c から選びましょう。

1. a   b   c

2. a   b   c

WRITING SECTION

> ✔ 「類似」のつなぎ言葉をうまく使うためのヒント
>
> 「類似」のつなぎ言葉とは、前に述べていることと、その後に続くことに共通点や類似点があることを明らかにするために使うつなぎ言葉のことです。

本文で取り上げた以外に、次のような「類似」を表すつなぎ言葉があります。

analogously（類似して）**as with**（の場合と同様）**by the same token**（同様に、その上）**for the same reason**（同じ理由から）**in a similar fashion/way/manner**（同じような方法［やり方・流儀］で）**in like fashion/manner**（似たような手法で）**in the same way/fashion/manner**（同じ方法で）**similar**（類似の）

「類似」を表すつなぎ言葉の具体的な使い方をみてみましょう。

1. I love spending time with my family, but **by the same token**, I also enjoy sharing time with my friends.
   （家族との時間も大好きですが、**それと同じように**、友人と時間を共有するのも楽しいです）

   same は（類似の物を指して）「同じ」「同様の」、ここで使われている token は、印（mark）象徴（symbol）証拠（evidence）のような意味です。前に述べた事柄と同様の理由や原因から生じていることを示す表現です。

2. John cooked sukiyaki **in the same way** his Japanese friend did.
   （ジョンは日本人の友人がしたのと**同じやり方で**スキヤキを作った）

   way は「方法」「やり方」、fashion は（広く行き渡っている、一般的な）「慣習」「様式」manner は「仕方」「態度」で、どれと組み合わせても同じ意味で使えます。「同じ理由で」だと **for the same reason** となります。

3. In an aerobics class, we do a warm-up at the beginning and a cool-down at the end **in like fashion**.
   （エアロビクスのクラスでは、最初にウォームアップ、最後にクールダウンを**同じ要領で**行う）

   この like は形容詞で「同様な」とか「ほぼ同じ」という意味です。in like の次には、名詞または代名詞がきます。

4. **As with** the previous projects, we need to collect all kinds of data for this one.
   （これまでのプロジェクト**と同様**、今回もあらゆるデータを集める必要がある）

   as with は 2 つ（以上）の物事や状況を比較して、その類似点や共通点を強調するときに使います。as with で 1 つの前置詞の役目をし、「〜の場合と同様」という意味になります。

本文に出ている analogous to（〜に似て）は、難しい語句に見えるかもしれませんが、これは analog（アナログ、類似のもの）に -ous（〜の性質がある）という接尾辞がついて analogous（類似した）となり、そのあとに to が続いて「〜に類似している」(similar to) という形容詞句になったものです。

I 次のそれぞれの英文にもっとも適したつなぎ言葉を下の選択肢から選びましょう。

1. The plot of the movie is (   ) to the original book.

2. All of my friends are (   ) important to me.

3. He likes action movies, and (   ), I like them too.

4. Tom does not like spicy food and avoids ordering Indian food at restaurants (   ).

> in like manner,   equally,   analogous to,   for the same reason,
>
> by the same token,   similar

II 与えられた語句を使って、次の日本語を英語にしましょう。

1. 私たちは昨年と同じやり方で調査結果を分析した。(in the same way)

   _____

2. チームは、試合に勝つために力を合わせる必要がある。同様に、グループプロジェクトも成功させるためには協力し合う必要がある。(analogously)

   _____

3. 姉は絵を描くのがとても好きで、同じように弟も楽器に夢中です。(similarly)

   _____

Ⅲ Let's practice transitions!

例文にならって、文を作ってみましょう。

例文

1. (a) Inexperienced public speakers often worry about making mistakes.

    (b) **Correspondingly**, many people experience similar problems when giving interviews.

Your original

(a) _____

(b) **Correspondingly**, _____

_____

2. **Like** a paragraph, a speech contains an introduction, organizing points, and a conclusion.

Your original

Like _____

_____

3. Listening to a speech read is **analogous to** watching a teacher read from a textbook.

Your original

_____ **analogous to** _____

_____

次のテーマで一つのパラグラフを英文で書きましょう。

テーマ：人前でうまく話すために私が準備していること

条 件：パラグラフライティングの手法を用いて書く。2つ以上の「類似」のつなぎ言葉を用いる。単語数は 100 words 程度とする。

本文では、人前でうまく話せるようになるための一例があげられていますが、あなたの場合は、どのような準備をするのがよいと思いますか。例をあげて自分の考えを1つのパラグラフにまとめてみましょう。出来上がったら、文書または口頭で発表しましょう。

Paragraph Title: _____

Introduction Sentence: _____

_____

Supporting Sentences: _____

_____

_____

_____

Concluding Sentence: _____

_____

他にもこんな「類似」のつなぎ言葉があります。

along similar lines（似たような路線の）**along the same lines**（同じ方法で）**as well as**（と同様に）**complementary to this**（これを補う形で）**in a similar vein**（同じように）**in equal measure**（同程度まで）**just as**（と全く同じように）

Brush-up Assignment

「類似」のつなぎ言葉を使った英文を、辞書や新聞、ネットなどで探して書き出してみましょう。

- _____

_____

- _____

_____

Chapter 15

Review of Paragraph Writing

パラグラフライティングのおさらいをする

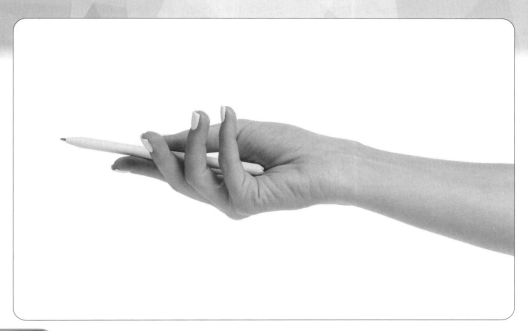

Aim

Transition Words & Phrases for EXCEPTION:

^A besides（以外に）^B other than（〜以外にも）^B apart from（〜は別として）^L aside from（の他に）

Core Idea: to review the paragraph writing process

WARM-UP

それぞれの語句に合う日本語を選んで、記号を（　）に入れましょう。

1. ^A serve as (　　　) **2.** ^A framework (　　　) **3.** ^A flow (　　) **4.** ^A move forward (　　　)

5. ^A distinctly (　　) **6.** ^B explicit (　　　) **7.** ^B bulk (　　) **8.** ^B confuse (　　　)

9. ^B entire (　　　) **10.** ^L assume (　　　)

---

a. を前に進める　　　b. を混乱させる　　　c. として機能する　　　d. 〜だと思う

e. はっきりと　　f. 明確な　　g. 流れる　　h. 全体の　　i. 大部分　　j. 枠組み

READING SECTION

Model Reading A

 58

Paragraphs serve as a logical framework for organizing ideas in English writing. A paragraph consists of three parts: an introduction, supporting sentences, and a conclusion. The more precise the structure, the easier for readers to understand a text. Paragraphs can be short or long, depending on the contents of the text. Paragraphs flow more naturally when transition words move the topic forward distinctly. Besides essays and papers, good paragraphs are essential for informal and business writing. As with any other piece of writing, the primary purpose of a paragraph is to share the author's message clearly and keep the reader engaged.

5

Notes ....
keep the reader engaged 読者を魅了し続ける

Ⅰ 本文を読んで、下線部に入るもっとも適切なものをa〜dより選びましょう。

The main purpose of a paragraph, _____ any other piece of writing, is to clearly convey the author's message and engage the reader.

    a. just like   **b.** different from   **c.** due to   **d.** in addition to

Ⅱ 本文の内容と一致するように、（　　）に適切な一語を書き入れましょう。

You can use short or long paragraphs. This (　　　　　　　　　) on the contents of the text you are writing.

Ⅲ Model Reading A と同じ内容になるように、次の英文を順に並べ替えましょう。

1. Writers can use short or long paragraphs based on what they are writing about.

2. Paragraphs help writers organize their ideas in English writing.

3. A clear paragraph structure makes it easier for readers to understand a text.

4. Using transition words in paragraphs makes the writing flow natural and helps advance the topic.

5. Each paragraph has three parts: an introduction, supporting sentences, and a conclusion.

(　　　) → (　　　) → (　　　) → (　　　) → (　　　)

Model Reading B

 59

Each part that makes up a paragraph plays a different but essential role in communicating with the reader. The introduction sentence explicitly introduces the main topic of the paragraph. Other than being clear, the topic should help the reader understand the paragraph's flow. Supporting sentences add information about the topic by providing examples or explicit reasons. The bulk of each paragraph consists of supporting sentences. However, adding too much explanation, apart from the necessary information, can confuse or bore the reader. Paragraphs end with a concluding sentence that briefly summarizes the main point of the entire paragraph.

I 本文を読んで、下線部に入るもっとも適切なものを a ～ d より選びましょう。

The end of the paragraph is a closing sentence that briefly _____ the main points of the entire paragraph.

    a. analyzes   **b.** extends   **c.** introduces   **d.** summarizes

II 本文の内容と一致するように、（   ）に適切な一語を書き入れましょう。

（   ） parts of each paragraph consist of supporting sentences.

III Model Reading B と同じ内容になるように、次の英文の下線部に適切な語句を書き入れましょう。

Main Idea: Each part of the paragraph serves a _____ but _____ role in communicating with the readers.

Supporting Details:

1. The first sentence in a paragraph is the _____, which aims to tell the reader what the _____ is about.

2. The paragraph's topic should be _____ and help the reader understand what will come _____.

3. The _____ sentences provide more information about the topic, usually through _____ or _____.

4. It is important to balance the amount of _____ and necessary _____ in a paragraph to make sure the _____ understands.

Conclusion: Close the paragraph with a _____ sentence that concisely _____ up the main point of the entire paragraph.

IV Reading A と Reading B にそれぞれ適したタイトルを英語で書きましょう。

Reading A : _____

Reading B : _____

LISTENING SECTION 〉

CD 60、61

I 次の会話文を聞いて空欄を埋めましょう。

A. Have you noticed that Japanese and English paragraphs serve different
(¹   )?

B. No, I assume that they are the same.

A. Aside from trying to be reader-friendly, the two styles are (²   )
different.

B. Can you give an example?

A. In English, a paragraph is used to introduce, (³   ), and conclude a
topic. In Japanese, a paragraph is (⁴   ) but plays a vital role as a
"separator" to break up groups of sentences that are too long.

B. I see! So, if I write an English paragraph without changing my style from Japanese,
it may be (⁵   ).

A. In addition, avoid the "ki-sho-ten-ketsu" format, in which a completely different
(⁶   ), called a "turn," is inserted before the conclusion!

B. Thanks for the tip! I'll make sure to keep that in mind.

Notes ⋯⋯
separator 区切り **ki-sho-ten-ketsu** 起承転結 (**introduction, development, turn, conclusion**)

II 質問を聞いて、正しい答えを a 〜 c より選びましょう。

1. a   b   c

2. a   b   c

WRITING SECTION

✔ **「除外」するつなぎ言葉をうまく使うためのヒント**

「〜を除いて」「〜は含まない」と言いたいときに使うのが「除外」のつなぎ言葉です。これらのつなぎ言葉は、一般的なルールやパターンからの例外や、ずれていることを示すために使用します。反論や例外を認めたり、ある文が普遍的でないことを示すために修飾したりするのに便利です。

本文で取り上げた以外では、次のような「除外」するつなぎ言葉があります。

except（[前置詞] 〜を除いて [接続詞] 〜ということを除いて [動詞] 〜を除外する）**except when**（〜でない限り）**exception**（例外）**exclude**（〜を排除する）**exclusive**（排他的な）**exclusive of**（〜を抜きにして）**not included**（含まれない）**omit**（〜を省略する）**with the exception of**（〜を除いて）

「除外」するつなぎ言葉 except の具体的な使い方をみてみましょう。

■ **前置詞の except の使用例**

1. The library is open every day **except** Mondays.
   （図書館は月曜日**を除く**毎日開館している）
   ある文に特定の人や物、事柄などが「含まれていない」ことを言うときに使います。名詞の前で使います。

2. Keep this door closed **except in** an emergency.
   （緊急時**以外は**、この扉を閉めておいてください）
   次に前置詞（on, at など）がきて、except [前置詞] ＋前置詞句の形で使います。

3. **Except for** a few joggers, the park is empty.
   （ジョギングをする人が数人いる**以外**、公園には誰もいない）
   文頭に except を使う場合は、except for を名詞の前に用います。

■ **接続詞の except の使用例**

4. This movie was perfect, **except that** I didn't like the leading actor.
   （この映画は、主演の俳優が私の好みでなかった**ことを除けば**、完璧だった）
   except that S ＋ V という形で、「〜という点を除いて」という意味で使います。

5. He looks handsome **except when** he snoozes.
   （居眠りをしている**時以外は**、彼はハンサムに見える）
   except の次に副詞節を導く接続詞（when, where, if, that など）と一緒に使います。
   except that の that は省略できますが、それ以外の接続詞を省略することはできません。

I 次のそれぞれの英文にもっとも適したつなぎ言葉を下の選択肢から選びましょう。文頭に来る語は大文字で書き始めましょう。

1. (   ) news and current events, I seldom watch television.

2. Be sure to attend the meeting (   ) when you are ill.

3. The price of this item is (   ) of consumption tax.

4. He was (   ) from the study room for snoring too loudly.

> exception,　except,　excluded,　besides,　aside from,　exclusive

II 与えられた語句を使って、次の日本語を英語にしましょう。

1. ランチはお一人様 1,000 円ですが、飲み物は含まれません。(not included)

_____

2. 何日か蒸し暑い日があった以外は、屋外での活動に最適な気候が続いている。
(with the exception of)

_____

3. 報告書は正確だったが、教授は一部の詳細を省略することを提案した。
(accurate, omitting)

_____

Ⅲ Let's practice transitions!

例文にならって、文を作ってみましょう。

> 例文

1. **Besides** essays and papers, good paragraphs are essential for informal and business writing.

> **Your original**

   Besides _____

2. **Other than** being clear, the topic should enable the reader to understand the flow of the paragraph.

> **Your original**

   Other than _____

3. Adding too much explanation, **apart from** the necessary information, can confuse or bore the reader.

> **Your original**

   _____ **apart from** _____

次のテーマで一つのパラグラフを英文で書きましょう。

> **テーマ**：パラグラフライティングのスキルはどのように向上したか
>
> **条　件**：パラグラフライティングの手法を用いて書く。2つ以上の「除外」のつなぎ言葉を用いる。単語数は 100 words 程度とする。

このテキストを通して、あなたは効果的な英語のパラグラフライティングのポイントを学び、その書き方を練習してきました。本書をやり終えるにあたって、あなたは自分のパラグラフライティングのスキルがどのように向上したと感じますか。10 点満点で自己評価して、その理由を含むパラグラフを書いてみましょう。出来上がったら、文書または口頭で発表しましょう。

Paragraph Title: ＿＿＿＿＿＿＿＿＿＿＿＿＿＿＿＿＿＿＿＿＿＿＿＿＿＿

Introduction Sentence: ＿＿＿＿＿＿＿＿＿＿＿＿＿＿＿＿＿＿＿＿＿

＿＿＿＿＿＿＿＿＿＿＿＿＿＿＿＿＿＿＿＿＿＿＿＿＿＿＿＿＿＿＿＿

Supporting Sentences: ＿＿＿＿＿＿＿＿＿＿＿＿＿＿＿＿＿＿＿＿＿＿

＿＿＿＿＿＿＿＿＿＿＿＿＿＿＿＿＿＿＿＿＿＿＿＿＿＿＿＿＿＿＿＿

＿＿＿＿＿＿＿＿＿＿＿＿＿＿＿＿＿＿＿＿＿＿＿＿＿＿＿＿＿＿＿＿

＿＿＿＿＿＿＿＿＿＿＿＿＿＿＿＿＿＿＿＿＿＿＿＿＿＿＿＿＿＿＿＿

Concluding Sentence: ＿＿＿＿＿＿＿＿＿＿＿＿＿＿＿＿＿＿＿＿＿＿

＿＿＿＿＿＿＿＿＿＿＿＿＿＿＿＿＿＿＿＿＿＿＿＿＿＿＿＿＿＿＿＿

他にもこんな「除外」のつなぎ言葉があります。

barring［前］～がなければ **excepting**（を除いて）**excluding**（～を除いて）**get rid of**（～を取り除く）**leave/leaving aside**（～はさて置いて）**make an exception of**（～を別扱いにする）**outside of**（～の他に）**save for**（［前置詞］～は別として）**without**（～なしで）

Brush-up Assignment

「除外」のつなぎ言葉を使った英文を、辞書や新聞、ネットなどで探して書き出してみましょう。

- ＿＿＿＿＿＿＿＿＿＿＿＿＿＿＿＿＿＿＿＿＿＿＿＿＿＿＿＿＿

＿＿＿＿＿＿＿＿＿＿＿＿＿＿＿＿＿＿＿＿＿＿＿＿＿＿＿＿＿＿

- ＿＿＿＿＿＿＿＿＿＿＿＿＿＿＿＿＿＿＿＿＿＿＿＿＿＿＿＿＿

＿＿＿＿＿＿＿＿＿＿＿＿＿＿＿＿＿＿＿＿＿＿＿＿＿＿＿＿＿＿

TEXT PRODUCTION STAFF

edited by	編集
Mitsugu Shishido	宍戸　貢
Fumi Matsumoto	松本　風見

English-language editing by	英文校閲
Bill Benfield	ビル・ベンフィールド

cover design by	表紙デザイン
Nobuyoshi Fujino	藤野 伸芳

text design by	本文デザイン
Nobuyoshi Fujino	藤野 伸芳

CD PRODUCTION STAFF

recorded by	吹き込み者
Karen Haedrich (AmerE)	カレン・ヘドリック（アメリカ英語）
Dominic Allen (AmerE)	ドミニク・アレン（アメリカ英語）

Tell Your Story! Using Transition Words in English Writing
つなぎ言葉でみがく英作文

2024年1月20日　初版発行
2024年2月15日　第2刷発行

著　者　中川 準治
　　　　Joe Alloway
　　　　Ayden Harris

発行者　佐野 英一郎

発行所　株式会社 成美堂
　　　　〒101-0052　東京都千代田区神田小川町3-22
　　　　TEL 03-3291-2261　FAX 03-3293-5490
　　　　https://www.seibido.co.jp

印刷・製本　倉敷印刷株式会社

ISBN 978-4-7919-7292-0　　　　　　　　Printed in Japan

17. but still ［成句］それにしても

18. admittedly ［副］明らかに、ご指摘通り

19. although it may be so ［成句］そうかもしれないが

20. while it is/may be true that ［成句］それは本当かもしれないが

16. even if ［成句］仮に～だとしても

17. but then again ［成句］しかしまた一方

18. with that in mind ［成句］その点（こと）を念頭に入れて

19. yet ［副］けれども

20. consequently ［副］必然的に

Chapter 9 GENERALIZING（一般化）

1. generally ［副］一般的に
2. commonly ［副］一般（的）に
3. in general ［成句］一般に
4. generally speaking ［成句］一般的には
5. usually ［副］通常
6. ordinarily ［副］通常
7. as a rule ［成句］原則的には
8. fundamentally ［副］根本的に
9. on the whole ［成句］全体的にみると
10. overall ［副］全般的に言えば ［形］総合的な
11. all in all ［成句］全体として見れば
12. all things considered ［成句］全体から見ると
13. typically ［副］総じて
14. by and large ［成句］総体的に
15. for the most part ［成句］ほとんどは
16. most often ［成句］ほとんどの場合
17. in most cases ［成句］大抵の場合
18. broadly speaking ［成句］大まかに言って
19. in the main ［成句］おおむね
20. without exception ［成句］例外なく

Chapter 11 PREPARATION（準備）

1. at first ［成句］初めは
2. first ［副］最初に ［形］最初の
3. firstly ［副］まず第一に
4. initially ［副］当初は
5. at the outset ［成句］冒頭で
6. the first step ［成句］最初の一歩
7. the initial stage ［成句］最初の段階
8. to start off ［成句］まず手始めに
9. as a first step ［成句］第一歩として
10. beforehand ［副］事前に
11. in advance of ［成句］～より前（先）に
12. prior to ［成句］～に先立って
13. ahead of time ［成句］前もって
14. preceding ［形］（名詞の前のみで）前の
15. in anticipation of ［成句］～を見込んで
16. with a view to ［成句］～を視野に入れて
17. with the aim of ［成句］～を目指して
18. plan ［動］計画を立てる
19. in preparation for ［成句］～に向けて
20. get ready for ［成句］～の準備をする

Chapter 10 LOGICAL RELATIONSHIP（論理的関係）

1. therefore ［副］その結果として
2. as a result ［成句］その結果
3. in consequence ［成句］その結果
4. hence ［副］このような訳で
5. accordingly ［副］従って
6. so ［副］従って
7. thus ［副］こういう訳で
8. for this reason ［成句］このような理由から
9. because of ［成句］～のために
10. since ［接］～なので
11. even though ［成句］～なのに
12. so that ［成句］～するために
13. in spite of ［成句］～にもかかわらず
14. based on that ［成句］それを踏まえて
15. nevertheless / none the less ［成句］それでもやはり

Chapter 12 DETAILS（詳細）

1. to be specific ［成句］具体的に言うと
2. specifically ［副］明確に、具体的には
3. in detail ［成句］詳しく
4. especially ［副］特に
5. particularly ［副］特に、とりわけ
6. notably ［副］特に、とりわけ
7. in particular ［成句］特に、とりわけ、とりたてて
8. in addition ［成句］その上
9. moreover ［副］その上に
10. including ［前］を含めて
11. besides ［副］その上、さらにまた
12. in fact ［成句］実は、実のところ
13. actually ［副］実際は
14. among others ［成句］数ある中でも、何よりも
15. above all else ［成句］何にもまして

16. in regard to ［成句］に関しては
17. additionally ［副］加えて
18. furthermore ［副］さらに
19. in other words ［成句］言い換えれば
20. list ［動］リストアップする

Chapter 13 RESTATEMENT（言い直し）
1. in other words ［成句］要するに
2. in brief ［成句］かいつまんで言うと、要するに
3. restate ［動］あらためて述べる
4. summarize ［動］要約する
5. in summary ［成句］要点としては
6. to put it differently/simply/another way ［成句］言い換えれば
7. stated another way ［成句］言い方を変えれば
8. put another way ［成句］言い換えれば
9. to put it another way ［成句］別の言い方をすれば
10. put differently ［成句］別の表現で言うと
11. briefly speaking ［成句］簡単に言うと
12. to put it simply ［成句］簡単に言えば
13. in short ［成句］要するに、手短に言えば
14. as discussed above ［成句］前述の通り
15. as discussed previously ［成句］前に述べたように
16. as noted above ［成句］上に指摘したように
17. as already noted ［成句］すでに言及してきたとおり
18. namely ［副］すなわち
19. basically ［副］基本的に見て
20. in essence ［成句］本質的には、根本的には

Chapter 14 SIMILARITY（類似）
1. similarly ［副］同様に
2. likewise ［副］同様に
3. as well as ［成句］と同様に
4. as with ［成句］と同様
5. by the same token ［成句］同様に、その上
6. along the same lines ［成句］同じ方法で
7. in the same way/fashion/manner ［成句］同じ方法で
8. for the same reason ［成句］同じ理由から
9. equally ［副］同じように
10. in a similar vein ［成句］同じように
11. correspondingly ［成句］これと同じように
12. just as ［成句］～と全く同じように

13. in equal measure ［成句］同程度まで
14. in a similar fashion/way/manner ［成句］同じような方法（やり方・流儀）で
15. analogously ［副］類似して
16. analogous to ［成句］～に似て
17. along similar lines ［成句］似たような路線の
18. in like fashion/manner ［成句］似たような手法で
19. similar ［形］類似の
20. like ［前］～に似た ［接］～のように ［形］似ている

Chapter 15 EXCEPTION（除外）
1. except ［前］～を除いて ［接］～ということを除いて ［動］除外する
2. with the exception of ［成句］～を除外して
3. excepting ［前］を除いて
4. besides ［前］～以外には
5. apart from ［成句］～以外は
6. other than ［成句］～以外の、以外にも
7. except for ［成句］～以外は
8. aside from ［成句］の他に
9. outside of ［成句］～の他に
10. save for ［前］～は別として
11. exclusive of ［成句］～を抜きにして
12. leave/leaving aside ［成句］～はさて置いて
13. make an exception of ［成句］～を別扱いにする
14. unless ［接］ただし～の場合は別だが
15. barring ［前］～がなければ
16. not included ［成句］含まれない
17. get rid of ［成句］～を取り除く
18. omit ［動］を省略する
19. without ［前］～なしで
20. exclude ［動］排除する